Olives

Olives

Cooking with Olives
and Their Oils

Ford Rogers

Ten Speed Press

Berkeley • Toronto

A Kirsty Melville Book

Ten Speed Press
PO Box 7123
Berkeley, California 94707
www.tenspeed.com

Conceived and produced by
Package Goods Incorporated
9 Murray Street
New York, NY 10007
A Quarto Company

Text by Ford Rogers
Cover photo and photographs on pages 4, 10, 12–13, 14, 44, 84, and 108 by Cary Wolinsky
Photographs on pages 1, 2, 20, 27, 32, 42–43, 60, 74, 98, and 106 by Jonathan Chester
All other photography by Tony Cenicola
Paintings by Linda St. Clair
Cover design by Toni Tajima
Interior design by Jan Melchior and Toni Tajima

Library of Congress Cataloging-in-Publication Data on file with the publisher.

First printing, 2002
Printed in China

1 2 3 4 5 6 7 8 9 10 — 05 04 03 02 01

Acknowledgments

First and foremost, I'd like to thank Steve Smith for his unwavering assistance

and inspiration, and my family for its continued encouragement.

I also want to thank all my friends who acted as willing guinea pigs, particularly

Martie LaBare, Mike McEvoy, John Morse, Alan and Jeanette Mittlesdorf,

Diane Foster, Sally Steinberg, John Scheffler, and Cathy Urmson.

Thanks to Carla Glasser and everyone at the Betsy Nolan Agency;

to Eric Jacobson, Lesley Ehlers, and Tony Cenicola for what I learned from

working with them; to Kristen Schilo, Tatiana Ginsberg, Lillien Waller,

Marta Hallett, and all at Packaged Goods; the folks at Ten Speed Press;

Jan Melchior; and all the merchants, clerks, trade representatives, and gourmands

especially Carrie Van Hise at Zona; Lily Genis at Wolfman Gold & Good Company;

the kind staff at Mackenzie-Childs Ltd; Liza Ratliff, Nancy McKay, and Billy Light at

Pier 1 Imports; and Kim Boriin, Keith LaPan, Margaux King, Sheila Rosart,

Peter Brodnitz, and Madeline Schilo for the use of their cooking wares.

Special thanks to Mrs. John Hay Whitney for the use of

Van Gogh's striking olive landscape; Marlyne Berger for the

rides across the Manhattan Bridge and the pleasure of her conversation;

and to Barbara Appel for taking such an interest.

Contents

"A taste older than meat,
older than wine.
A taste as old as cold water."
—Lawrence Durrell

Introduction

Throughout history, many great accomplishments have come to us from the Mediterranean—the time-proven model for Western democracy, breathtaking works of art, inspiring forms of architecture, soul-stirring sounds of music, and a truly international cuisine, which has at its heart olives and their oil. No cuisine on earth has proven so healthy and body-friendly.

What spices were to the East, olives and olive oil were and are to the nations of the Mediterranean—and then some. The inhabitants of such places often see olives as gifts from God, or the gods, because they grow in places and climates not suited to many other crops. These people have known for generations that olives would nourish them in hard times when there was nothing else to eat. Because of their long-believed and recently proven health benefits, they just might be nature's most perfect creations.

The people of the Mediterranean and Southern Europe have eaten a diet plentiful in olives and olive oil for thousands of years and consequently have one of the lowest heart disease rates. Those of us elsewhere, who have gotten most of our fat from animals in the past, have in the last two decades begun to realize the effect it's been having on us. Olive oil is a way out of our unhealthy habits, and is good for us and good tasting.

In this book we will follow the history of olive cultivation and explore the cultures that grew up around and because of it. You will find descriptions of what to look for when buying olive oil, along with the different types and ways to use them.

Last but not least are the recipes—appetizers like *Garlic Shrimp with Atalanta Olives*; starters and soups, including *Tomato Soup with Red Wine and Kalamata Olives*; drinks such as a *Retsina Spritzer with Greek Olives*; sauces for pasta, meat, poultry, vegetables, and fish; vegetarian dishes such as *Fresh Herb Risotto with Naphlion Olives*; seafood preparations, including *Herbed Swordfish with Naphlion Olives*; meat dishes such as *Beef, Tomato, and Niçoise Olive Ragout*; and even baked goods starring *Most Memorable Madeleines*.

Olives come in dozens of types. Their tastes range from salty to bland, from sour to almost sweet. Their colors range from pale gold to jet black. More methods have been used to cure them than you could sample in a lifetime, from ashing to make them sweet, to dry-salting to make them strong; from brining to tame them, and to Chinese dry-curing with salt, sugar, and licorice.

With olives, we have a nearly perfect food—a fruit with dozens of varieties and flavors that allow for a multitude of uses, whose oil is healthful, delicious, and seemingly limitless in its uses. Use some today and every day. Pick a recipe and start cooking. Become privy to the secret of Mediterranean happiness, health, and longevity.

PART ONE

The Olive Observed

CHAPTER I

The Well-Rounded Olive:
From Past to Present

THE OLIVE
IN HISTORY
AND
MYTH

Since its earliest cultivation by man, *Olea europaea*, the olive, has been much more than just a food crop. Because of the areas in which it is cultivated and the important effects it's had on the lives of the inhabitants of those areas, the olive has been surrounded throughout history with myths to explain it, commercial ventures to promote it, and political actions to protect it.

There is much archaeological evidence available today to prove the olive's integral part in every aspect of Mediterranean life for centuries. From 3,000-year-old mummies preserved with olive oil and bowls of cured olives found in pharaohs' tombs in Egypt, to olives preserved in the ruins of Pompeii; from depictions in 2,000-year-old Egyptian art, to olive-leaf fossils discovered in Pliocene era deposits in Italy and Paleolithic strata in North Africa; the olive has been an essential element in day-to-day life.

One theory holds that the ancestor of the cultivated olive tree originated in Asia Minor and spread from there to other areas in the Mediterranean basin. Other theories claim lower Egypt, the Atlas Mountains, parts of Southern Europe, or the entire Mediterranean as the olive's birthplace. Since everyone except the Assyrians and Babylonians seems to have been aware of the olive, its growth was widespread long before there was a written history to record its origins.

It would seem the cultivation of the olive began with breeding experiments about 6,000 to 7,000 years ago in Crete and Asia Minor. From there, its use spread steadily in all directions, getting major boosts from the Minoans, and later the Phoenicians, who disseminated the olive widely and began a lucrative trade in olive oil. Most of the ancient ships discovered in the Mediterranean in recent years have been full of amphoras—large clay jars whose main use was the transport of olive oil.

The olive apparently made it to the Greek mainland somewhere between the 14th and 12th centuries BCE, to Northern Africa and Sicily in the sixth century BCE, and to mainland Italy around 600 BCE. By the time of their empire's great expansion, the Romans found the olive tree already long cultivated by the Berbers of North Africa. But even so, they introduced it wherever it was not already known. The Romans were responsible for taking the olive to what is now Southern France and from there throughout Gaul, as well as to Sardinia.

The olive tree had been introduced to Spain by the Phoenicians, around 1,000 BCE, but it was not widely cultivated until the arrival of the Roman Scipio in 212 BCE. The Moors further influenced Spanish olive cultivation with the introduction of their own varieties and methods in the eighth century CE.

With their voyages to the Americas in the early 15th century, the Spanish—mainly priests and monks—transported the olive to Central and South America, and later to California.

In more recent years, the olive's cultivation has spread even further, as far as Australia, South Africa, and China—wherever the soil and climate permit.

There are those who argue that the olive is the reason for the Roman Empire. They speculate that the need for oil was so great, for everything from lighting lamps, to oiling skin, to healing bodies, to greasing axles and cooking food, that continuous expansion was required to fill the need. In fact, the Romans were the inventors of the screw press for extracting oil, a technology that is only now beginning to find competition. Additionally, the Romans were great lovers of pickled and cured olives, which they thought were aphrodisiacs when eaten in large quantities.

Because of its slow initial growth and the effect damage has on the output of a fruit-bearing tree, the olive has long been a symbol of peace. But the symbolism and myth surrounding the olive goes much further than that and occurs in every culture that cultivates it.

In every culture where the olive was cultivated, it was raised to the status of a sacred tree, an object of veneration and an important asset worth defending. Rulers' scepters and thrones were made of olive wood. In virtually every religion ever extant in the Mediterranean, its oil has been used in ceremonies, for anointing kings and priests, the newly dead or the recently born. And each of those religions has a mythology to explain the olive, its origins and properties.

Six thousand years ago, the Egyptians believed that Isis, wife of Osiris, the supreme god of their pantheon, had taught people how to grow and use olives.

Early Judeo-Christian legend says that Adam, on his deathbed, asked for the oil of mercy which the Lord had given him for his own and all peoples' redemption. He sent his son Seth to the angel that guarded Eden. The angel gave Seth three seeds from the tree of knowledge and told him to place them in Adam's mouth after he died. He did so and buried his father. From the site three trees grew: a cedar, a cypress, and an olive tree—the Mediterranean's main arboreal specimens.

The New Testament also mentions the olive trees that stood silent witness to events in the life of Jesus, especially those that surrounded him in the Garden of Gethsemane on the Mount of Olives and those among which he was laid to rest.

The Koran speaks of the olive as food and condiment for the table. It compares Allah to "the light of the heavens and earth," to a niche which enshrines a lamp "within a crystal of starlike brilliance," a lamp "lit from a blessed olive tree neither eastern or western."

Whatever their religious beliefs, the people of the Mediterranean have viewed their olive trees reverentially. When Solon enacted laws protecting olive trees in Greece in the sixth century, making it a capital offense to kill one or cut it down, they became more protected than slaves (and even children and women in most places). An oath of chastity was required for those who harvested the fruit for the duration of the harvest. It's claimed that only virgins and abstinent men were allowed to work in the groves.

Only things of great importance develop such mythologies and rules surrounding their use and care. The history of the olive is also the story of people living in hard times in often inhospitable places, while protecting and nurturing the most useful and beneficial source of sustenance in their world. Today, we still enjoy the bounty from centuries of their labor.

A WORD ABOUT THE RECIPES

There are certain factors that hold true for all the recipes in this book. To avoid repeating them endlessly, they are compiled here for easy reference.

First of all, olives have sodium. They have all been cured in salt, solid or dissolved, to some extent. For this reason I have noted in each recipe to salt to taste. Always sample before salting, either the olive being used or the dish. I find pepper to also be a very personal spice and therefore, suggest adding pepper to your own liking as well.

If any given olive is just too salty for you, it can be made somewhat less so by simmering in water for around 10 minutes before using in the recipe. A small amount can also be removed simply by rinsing the olives before using.

When a recipe calls for a "nonreactive" pan, this means one fabricated from substances that will not react with ingredients such as citrus juice, wine, or vinegar and cause an "off," metallic taste. The primary reactive metals are iron and aluminum. Iron is fine to use, if it is enameled. Aluminum is all right if it has been anodized.

In some areas different varieties of olives are impossible to get except by mail order. So, in the introduction to each recipe alternative olive choices are listed. I used a wide range of olives in these recipes, often because the taste of a particular variety is most appropriate to the dish, but some-times, to encourage the use of many different kinds of olives. Feel free to mix and mingle olives and olive types to your imagination's delight. But in those recipes where I have suggested a certain type be avoided, it is with good reason.

Generally my suggestions will involve avoiding bitter varieties in certain dishes. This is because the bitterest black olives tend to taste even more bitter with long cooking or after sitting in a dish overnight as leftovers, often making the entire dish bitter. Some people like a bitter taste, and some of the bitter olives, such as oil-cured, are among my favorites. That doesn't mean they always work well in every recipe, unfortunately.

Several recipes require small amounts of tomato paste. I suggest you buy a tube of tomato paste and keep it in your refrigerator.

I have also used a great many fresh herbs, noting appropriate substitutions of dried ones. If it's at all possible to use fresh herbs, your taste buds will appreciate the flavorful difference.

The goal of all of this is to make your experience in the kitchen with olives as easy and pleasant as possible. Much of the delight one experiences from an incredible dish can be muted if you've had to jump through hoops to prepare it. I hope, above all, you enjoy cooking with olives and olive oil, and experience the greatest pleasure from the fruits of your labor.

CHAPTER 2

From the Tree to the Table

GROWING THE OLIVE

The olive is a member of the botanical order of the Ligustrals, the *Oleaceae* family, with relatives such as jasmine, lilac, and ash. The *Olea* genus itself contains some 30 different species found all over the world. The one we are interested in here is *Olea europaea*, the cultivated olive tree we know today.

Some believe that *Olea europaea* was adapted from its scruffy cousin, the oleaster, or wild olive. But the oleaster is now classified as a subspecies of *Olea europaea* and tends to abandon its wild appearance and enlarge in fruit size when tended, indicating it to be a regressed form of the cultivated variety, rather than an ancestor.

The origin of our modern-day olive tree is lost in the distant past, before recorded history, but it seems to have become a cultivated crop about 6,000 to 7,000 years ago. Since then dozens of varieties have been developed, many of them lost over the centuries, leaving about 75 major cultivated varieties today.

The olive is a fruit. It is a drupe, like a cherry or peach, with a thick skin, meaty pulp, and a single central seed or pit. But it has a lower sugar and a higher oil content than other drupes, and a bitter component (oleuropein) makes it inedible straight off the tree. The olive tree is native to temper-ate-hot climates, particularly the Mediter-ranean. Outside these areas, it will not fruit properly, if it grows at all.

The olive tree can withstand tempera-tures as low as 45° to 50°F (8° to 10°C) for extended periods, even lower for brief peri-ods. In fact, for proper fruit production, it requires short blasts of temperatures close to freezing to induce vegetative rest. During the summer months, the olive tree can with-stand temperatures that are quite high, as well as a lack of moisture, though slightly prolonged dryness can affect the yield. The tree does not like a lot of moisture either, and high humidity encourages disease.

The trees' trunks are initially cylindrical, but over time they develop "veins" and look like tied bundles of trunks, or even human figures or faces. The height of the trunk depends on how it is pruned.

Orchards, the most common form of growing area for olives, are planned accord-ing to space available and space needed for each tree. Pruning helps train the trees to the shape of the area provided for them. The methods of pruning are therefore linked to the type of orchard and its age. After pruning at the end of the growing sea-son and a period of rest, the trees put out new twigs and leaves, followed by long-stalked clusters of hermaphrodite flowers, about 2 percent to 3 percent of which become harvestable fruit.

Besides its value as a cash crop, the olive tree further serves an ecological purpose. Planted largely in places with poor soil and little rainfall, in areas where few other plants can survive, and on rocky terrain or hillsides where the topsoil has been washed away, the tree, with its shallow, wide-spreading roots, plays an important role in combating further erosion.

Olive trees take between five and 10 years to reach fruit-bearing age, and can live for more than 600 years. Currently there are about 800 million olive trees planted worldwide, and the number continues to grow as the demand for olives and their oils increases.

PRODUCING THE OLIVE

There are some 800 million olive trees planted on Earth at this time. The main area of olive production remains the Mediterranean, the olive's birthplace and cradle, and home to 93 percent of those trees.

Although there are international standards of growing, processing, and labeling olives and their oils, differences among countries remain. Because growing conditions, altitudes, and space considerations vary, localized means of handling olives have arisen.

Because the olive's history in each country has been different, its status varies from border to border. Despite yearly increases in production and demand, 92 percent of the oil, and 80 percent of the table olives produced are still consumed in the country in which they originated.

Greece

Yearly figures vary somewhat, but Greece is usually the world's third largest producer of olive oil and the second largest producer of table olives. Greeks are consistently the world's largest consumers of olive oil, at about 6 gallons (23 *liters*) per person per year, compared with only one-third of a pint (*one-fifth of a liter*) per person per year in the United States.

The olives are almost all grown in small, individual family orchards. These families take advantage of centralized, cooperative pressing plants. Olives for oil are delivered by the individual growers to the centralized plants where they are pressed, with the cooperatives keeping a portion of the oil to pay for the process and the remainder going back to the growers, primarily for their own use.

Greek olive oils are generally affordable and easy to find. The bulk of the crop has gone to refined oils in the past, much of which is exported to Italy for blending with virgin oils. Many of the oils you buy which are labeled "product of Italy," were actually grown in Greece. In recent years, Greece has begun to produce extra virgin and virgin oils of better quality. Currently the best oils are grown in Crete and the Messina, and the Laconia and Zante regions.

Greece grows more kinds of olives than just about any other country, including Kalamata, Coronkeiki, Atalanta, Naphlion, Valonolia, Royal (or Royal Victoria), Agrinion, Thrubolea, Elitses, Conservolea, Adramitiki, Salona, Lianolia, Mastoidis, Amfissa, Mirtolia, and Ionian varieties.

Italy

Well known and respected for their full, fruity flavors, Italian extra virgin oils are consistently the best in the world.

The majority of olive cultivation takes place in the central and southern areas of the country, as well as on Sicily and Sardinia. The most productive areas are the Apulian and Calabrian regions, the heel and toe of the boot, respectively. The most consistently high quality oils come from the hilly regions of Tuscany and Abruzzi in the central part of the country. But excellent oils come from many growing regions.

As in Greece, much olive cultivation is done on small family farms which join together in cooperatives to press, bottle, and export their oil. Unlike Greece, there are a number of estate farms with large holdings.

The Italians manage to use about 2.6 gallons (10 *liters*) of oil per person per year. However, they have a problem that's the opposite of the one the Greeks have. While Greece has been unable to manufacture sufficient high grade oils, Italy has had a problem producing enough in the lower grades. That's why they import so much Greek oil to blend with their own. In fact, the Italians now import more than they export.

Italy produces dozens of olive varieties for oil and table consumption. Among the varieties grown are: Baresi, Gaeta, Sinopolese, Nocellara, Cucco, Ascolana, Apulian, Cerignola, Sicilian, San Remo, Coratina, Frantoio, Nicastrese, Pasola, Carolea, Itrana, Lecino, and Cellina Dinardo.

Spain

From year to year, Spain and Italy consistently top the list of olive oil producers, alternating between the first- and second-place designation. There are nearly 200 million olive trees in Spain, occupying 4.9

million acres of land (*2 million hectares*). The most prolific regions for oil production are Jaen and Cordoba, both in the south-central part of the country.

The Instituto Nacional de Denominaciones de Origen, the national organization which governs the olive oil industry, currently recognizes four labels of origin for oils of distinctively high quality and good taste: Borjas Blancas, Siurana, Sierra de Segura, and Baena. These areas of Catalonia and Andalusia produce the most consistently exceptional oils in Spain.

There are small growers and farms in Spain, but the bulk of Spanish olive cultivation is done by large company-owned orchards and processed in enormous quantities.

Besides being one of the two largest producers of olive oil, Spain is consistently the largest producer of table olives in the world. Among the varieties grown are: Manzanilla, Verdena, Lechin, Blanqueta, Gordal, Navadillo, Cacerena, Cornezuelo, Farga, Arbequina, Picudo, Hojiblanca, Picual, and Verdial de Badojoz.

France

France is one of the smallest producers of olive oil, but the bulk of what it produces is high-quality extra virgin oil. It's famous for its so-called "Lady Oils," which are delicate, sophisticated, and go for high prices.

Olive cultivation in France is confined to the south, southeast, and Corsica, with the bulk coming from a strip along the Mediterranean, from the Italian border to Spain, with the centers of production in Nyons and around the Vallée des Baux. They have developed innumerable methods for curing and flavoring olives. Among the various types are: Picholine, Rougeon, Nyons, Grossanne, Coucourelle, La Tanche, Salonenque, Lucques, Cailletier, Niçoise, and Redoutant.

Other Mediterranean Countries

Twenty percent of the population of Tunisia is engaged in the cultivation and production of the country's 50 million olive trees. Ranking fourth in world production, Tunisia exports half of the 132,000 tons (*120,000 tonnes*) of oil produced annually. Though the Tunisians grow a number of good table olives, they use them locally and haven't yet exported them.

Morocco, the seventh largest producer of olive oil, has also developed a well-deserved reputation for its outstanding table olives. The Moroccan Picholine is among them.

Turkey has made great strides toward improved production and promotion of its olive oil industry. Turkey produces refined oils primarily, and now ranks fifth in worldwide production. Here again, table olives are produced exclusively for local consumption.

Portugal has great terrain and the right climate for its 50 million trees, the same number as in Tunisia. But due to different growing conditions and methods, Portugal only produces a third as much oil. Varieties grown there include Carrasquenha, Redondil, Galega, and Verdeal.

Outside the Mediterranean

The olive has spread all over the world in recent decades and small amounts of oil and table olives are now produced in China, Chile, Peru, Brazil, Mexico, Angola, South Africa, Uruguay, Afghanistan, Australia, and California. The California industry, which has made its name with canned ripe olives and pimento-stuffed Manzanilla olives, is a major producer of table olives—one of the few crops in the U.S. still grown on small to medium-sized farms. California has only recently begun serious oil production, with orchards now in the Napa Valley, among other places. The U.S., however, isn't a member of the International Olive Oil Council and doesn't follow its guidelines on labeling. It has been the California producers' habit in the past to label all nonrefined oil as "extra virgin," with no organoleptic assessment made.

CURING
THE
OLIVE

No one knows who first thought to cure olives to make them edible, or how he or she came up with the idea. One theory claims that olives, growing on the cliffs above the Aegean, dropped into the ocean, where they soaked in the salty water for several days. They might then have floated out to sea to be found by a sailor or a fisherman who tasted them.

One-tenth of the world's olive production escapes the oil presses and is earmarked for table consumption. Except for a couple of varieties that ferment and sweeten as they ripen, olives are inedible as they come off the tree, due to the bitter component oleuropein, which is found only in olives. Though oleuropein has a very unpleasant taste, it is not hazardous to human health. All the methods of curing so far devised are designed to separate that component and produce an olive with a delicious taste.

The olives chosen for curing are usually of an appropriate size, medium to large, and more or less spherical in shape. The most marketable ones have at least a 4 percent sugar content, come easily away from their stones, and have at least a five-to-one flesh-to-stone ratio (Niçoise are notable exceptions). Their skins are thin, yet strong enough to resist blows and the actions of alkalis and brines.

Green olives are almost always harvested by hand, and those destined for the table should be undamaged and taken the day they're harvested to begin one of two types of processing, "Spanish style," which involves fermentation, and "Picholine" or "American style," which does not.

Spanish style involves treating the olives in a weak alkali solution to remove the bit-

ter oleuropein and transform the sugars so that they will aid fermentation. They remain in the alkali until it has penetrated two-thirds of the way into the flesh, then they're washed and placed in containers which are subsequently filled with brine. Traditionally, wooden barrels have been used, but more recently, larger lined tanks have become popular. Once the olives have properly fermented in the brine, they should keep for a long time. Usually they are classified, packed in barrels or glass or metal containers, and a new brine is added before sealing and shipping.

For the Picholine or American style of processing used on many olives in the South of France, Morocco, and Algeria, the oleuropein is leached out by leaving them in an alkali solution for eight to 12 hours, until the alkali has penetrated three-quarters of the way into the flesh. During the next 24 hours, they are rinsed repeatedly. Then they are put into a 3 percent brine solution, which is gradually raised to 10 percent. Within eight to 10 days, they are ready for marketing. They are washed repeatedly and packed in a new brine.

Semiripe olives have a process all their own, which is a mainstay of the California olive industry. The well-known canned, ripe California olives, are processed in this fashion. The olives, picked before they're fully ripe, are placed in a 2 percent alkali solution in large cement tanks. They are aerated with compressed air. Repeated soaking and aerating allow the alkali to penetrate all the way to the stone. The olives are then thoroughly washed before being placed in a solution of ferrous gluconate (a nutritious substance used in iron supplements) to darken them. After steaming or pasteurization, they are put into a 3 percent brine solution for two to three days, before sorting them by size, packing them in cans with a new brine, sterilizing, and shipping them.

USING
AND STORING
OLIVES

Olives come in a full array of colors, from pale gold to jet black and in every size from big to small. There are sweet olives, sour olives, fruity, earthy, nutty, salty, bitter, bland, and just about everything in between. You can buy them in jars, cans, wooden or plastic barrels, or from a crock in a market; packed in brine, vinegar, oil, vacuum-packed dry, or dressed in just about any seasoning. They come pitted, unpitted, cracked, sliced, chopped, seasoned, stuffed, broken, or ground into a paste. Your choice isn't even restricted by where you live, because you can mail order olives.

Olive nomenclature can get confusing, it's true. They can be named for their place of origin, such as Nyons or Kalamata; for their variety, like Picholine or Agrinion; for the method used to cure them, such as California Sicilian-style or cracked green; or even for a combination of things, like cracked Provençal or Moroccan oil-cured. But none of that matters if you buy them some place where

you can taste them first. The bottom line is the taste—you either like them or you don't.

After you buy olives, and you somehow manage not to eat them all at one sitting, how you keep them becomes very important. Olives should always be kept moist, either in brine, plain water, or drizzled with olive oil. They may be kept at a cool room temperature for a week or two in olive oil, but less for ash-cured varieties like Bella di Cerignola and Baresi Dolci. If you want to keep them longer than that, you should keep them in brine or refrigerated. Olives should always be eaten at room temperature or above, never cold. They can be warmed by letting them sit at room temperature for an hour or two, or by gently heating them in a little olive oil in a pan over a low flame.

If your olives came in a brine, never discard the brine until all the olives are eaten. Return any uneaten olives to the brine, and, if they were in a jar when you bought them, refrigerate any leftovers. You can make your own brine by dissolving about a tablespoon of salt to each pint of clean water. Olives will keep at room temperature in your homemade brine for about a month.

Olives that come from brine should always be rinsed before eating or cooking. If you buy your olives from a crock in a market, ask for some of the brine they were in, or drizzle them with a little extra virgin olive oil to keep them from drying out.

Some people have a problem with olives because they can be high in sodium. This is a result of their curing, not because of the olives themselves. If you are on a severely sodium-restricted diet, you should choose your olives very carefully. For the rest of us, even those olives highest in sodium can be used without negative effects, if we use them carefully.

There are a few things you can do to lessen the sodium content of even the saltiest olives. First, rinse all olives that have been in brine before eating or using them. Soaking in clean, clear water for about three days, taking care to change the water daily, also helps some. The most effective way, however, is to use the saltiest olives in cooking, adding no additional salt, but using the sodium they contain as the salt for the dish.

Another problem some people have with olives is that they think they are too bitter. Oil- or dry-cured olives tend to be the most bitter. If you inadvertently purchase olives that are too bitter for you, don't throw them out. You may simmer them in water for 10 to 15 minutes to remove some of the bitterness, or you can dress them with oil, fresh herbs, and garlic to balance their strong flavor.

Another misconception people have about olives is that they're fattening. In truth they are between four and 18 calories apiece, depending on their size—that's less than the average cracker. They also contain a relatively high proportion of essential amino acids, like leucine, aspartic acid, and glutaminic acid; unsaturated fatty acids, such as oleic acid; appreciable quantities of vitamins E and A, and beta carotene; and minerals, like calcium and magnesium.

PITTING OLIVES

If you're eating olives out of a bowl, you know what to do with the pits. But if you're cooking with olives, pitting them makes your dish easier to eat, with less work for your guests and less danger of damaging their teeth. Should you choose to serve the olives unpitted in a prepared dish, as they usually do in the Mediterranean, always warn your guests.

Some olives can be found in jars already pitted, such as California ripe black, Manzanilla, and occasionally Sevillano or Queen. The only European olive commonly sold pitted is the Atalanta, but sometimes you may come across a crock of "pitted green French olives" or other such oddities. If such prepitted olives are important to you, get them while you can. You may never see them again.

If you need another kind of olive pitted, you'll have to do it yourself. The quickest and easiest way of pitting I've found is with a cherry pitter, or *denoyauteur*. Unfortunately, pitters only work on olives that are approximately cherry-sized, and don't cling too tenaciously to their pits. I've had success using a pitter on Alphonso, Greek black, Greek green, Kalamata, Lebanese black, and Manzanilla olives.

The juicier dry-cured olives and the cracked varieties can be pulled apart. The harder dry-cured varieties and some smaller kinds such as Niçoise, Picholine, or Gaeta can sometimes be started by pinching them by the ends between the thumb and forefinger until they split, then pulling them apart. Sometimes you'll be successful if you cut around the equator of each olive and turn the two hemispheres in opposite directions. If neither of these methods works, lay several down on a board or countertop and mash down as if you were peeling garlic. This usually splits the flesh and loosens the pit, allowing them to be separated.

If you need small olives with not too hard flesh, such as Niçoise, pitted but still intact, the only way to pit them is to use a thin, one-eighth of an inch thick metal or bamboo rod, such as a skewer. Carefully and slowly push in one end of the olive and the pit out the other, while you hold the olive between two fingers. The pit can deflect the end of your stick, so watch your fingers, use the nonpointed end if you can, and go slowly. On the very hardest of all, the Bella di Cerignolas, the California Sicilian-style, and the Sevillanos or Queens, your only option is cutting the meat from the pit with a paring knife.

Try several different methods of pitting olives and see which one works best for specific olives and for you. If all else fails, just inform your guests that you're having a traditional Mediterranean dining experience, and that the olives still have pits in them— so be careful.

CHAPTER 3

Nature's Most Essential Oil

PRESSING THE OLIVE

All the characteristics an olive oil ends up with are determined by the variety, climate, growing conditions, harvesting methods, and the method and speed with which it is pressed. The first requirement in the pressing process is whole, sound olives. The way those olives are obtained and the way they are treated at every step in the extraction process effects the end result.

Methods have changed very little since the earliest days of oil production, and those changes have been more in efficiency rather than in the actual process. The basic requirements for excellent oils remain the same: use good olives and do as little as possible to alter them.

The olives must be clean when they enter the mill. They must then be sorted according to variety, condition, and how they are obtained (i.e., picked from the tree or off the ground). Some producers leave in some leaves to produce a greener oil.

Since storage for any length of time causes the olives to heat up and begin to ferment, deteriorating the oil's odor and taste, the more quickly they are crushed, the better.

Originally, crushing was done by hand in stone basins, but later developments produced larger millstones driven by animals, then steam, gasoline, and finally, electrical engines. Hammer crushers have come into use more recently. These rolling stones, or hammers, crush the olives, pits and all, to a paste. Blades scrape the paste up and it is then homogenized in special, temperature-controlled mixers. To avoid fermentation, temperature must be controlled and attended to every step of the way.

The olive paste is spread out on fiber mats or filter discs, which are stacked and then pressed. The screw press, invented by the Romans, has been the method of choice for 2,000 years and is still used today, although the hydraulic press is increasing in popularity. These modern hydraulic presses exert pressures of up to 110 to 143 square pounds (*50 to 65 kilograms per centimeter square*) on the paste, causing the oil and vegetable waters to seep out. The seeping liquids are collected in decanters. It takes about 11 pounds (*five kilograms*) of olives to produce four and a quarter cups (*one liter*) of oil.

The oils that seep out before the hydraulic pressure reaches 88 square pounds (*40 kilograms per centimeter square*) are usually decanted separately, because of their superior quality, and sold as the highest-priced extra virgin oil.

In the past, the decanted liquids were separated by gravity, but more recently centrifuges, revolving at 6,000 to 7,000 rpm's, provide more rapid separation. The resulting oil can be filtered, if desired, but that's not necessary. These high quality virgin oils, around 20 percent of the total oil output, can be bottled as is, as extra, fine, or ordinary virgin oils; blended with one another to achieve specific desired taste characteristics; or blended with inferior oils to give them an olive oil taste.

Because of damage, pest infestation, poor harvesting or processing, or less than ideal growing conditions, some virgin oils end up with less than desirable taste, odor, or acidity levels. These are called lampante virgin oils. To make them more marketable, they must undergo a refining process, in which they are neutralized with alkaline bleaches to remove excess free fatty acids, then decolorized with bleaching clays and active carbon, deodorized with reheated steam, and finally winterized by cooling and filtering to remove clouding triglycerides. This treated oil has no appreciable taste, odor, or color. It is usually mixed with extra or fine virgin oil to give it some character. It must be sold labeled "olive oil."

The oil left in the olive paste after the first pressing is the source of another refined oil, olive pomace oil. In earlier days, the paste was first mixed with warm water, then re-pressed to extract more oil. By the end of the 19th century, however, organic solvents had become available for entraining the fat, with a subsequent distillation to release it. Earlier solvents were often quite harsh and produced oil only appropriate for industrial uses, but more recent solvents, particularly hexane, make it possible to obtain good potable oil from the oil left in the paste.

The pomace should be processed as soon as possible to obtain oil with the lowest possible acidity level. It is first dried with warm air until it has attained 10 percent moisture, then further crushed to allow for maximum contact with the solvent. The pomace is placed in tanks, where it is injected with solvents, which are run through it repeatedly. Steam is added to remove the solvent residue by evaporation. The oil is then separated from any remaining water, and the olive pomace oil must then begin the process of refinement described above for lampante virgin oils.

The pomace oil is then blended with virgin oil to produce "olive oil" or used for industrial purposes, such as cosmetic manufacture.

Although the process of pressing olives to obtain their oils can be intricate, an understanding of production makes it clear why some olive oils cost so much more than others, and why the relatively small percentage of olive oil that earns the classification of "extra virgin" can be so expensive by the time it reaches the store. Ironically, though this superior oil does not require as much production as oils earning a lesser classification, it requires perfect olives and the greatest possible speed in production. The result seems to be worth it, however. The oil produced is the most natural, least processed oil in the world—made from freshly squeezed olives, then bottled, and ready for our enjoyment.

USING
AND STORING
OLIVE OIL

It's time to stop thinking of olive oil as an expensive commodity just for use in salads. While this may be the best way to use top-of-the-line extra virgin oils, it's hardly the whole picture. The less expensive oils, those labeled "virgin," or simply "olive oil," can successfully be substituted for any fat used in any recipe and will make the recipe healthier and tastier.

With 115 calories per tablespoon, the same as other cooking oils, olive oil can actually save you calories, because its more assertive flavor and aroma allow you to use less than you would other oils. Like all other vegetable oils, olive oil has no cholesterol. Since dietary fats are necessary, even if you're on a strict diet, you must intake some fat. Olive oil is the perfect choice because it's all natural, it's the healthiest and most easily absorbed edible fat (with *14 grams per tbsp*, but only *2 grams* of saturated fat), and a little can go such a long way.

Olive oil is the only cooking and salad oil in the world that offers a seemingly limitless variety of natural flavors from which to choose. From bland and innocuous to robust and full-flavored, from fruity to earthy, delicate to buttery, from nutty to peppery, or zesty to sweet—whatever you want from olive oil, tastewise, it can provide.

Obviously the more flavorful, more expensive extra virgin oils should be used where their flavor can be most appreciated. Since their flavors break down at higher temperatures (starting at 140°F, or *59°C*), and have a low smoking point (around 300°F, or *149°C*), expensive flavorful oils are wasted in frying, sautéing, and baking. Use them on salads or breads, and for drizzling on cooked dishes just before serving. Oils labeled "olive oil" are much more appropriate for cooking as their smoking points are much higher (406°F to 468°F, or *208°C to 242°C*). Their taste isn't a factor and they contain the same healthful properties that the more expensive oils do. They are perfect for frying because, unlike other cooking oils, olive oil coats the food rather than being absorbed, thus sealing in the food's flavor and producing a thin, crisp crust with no greasiness. Because it's stable at higher temperatures and contains antioxidants, you can filter olive oil after frying and use it up to four or five times. Even if you've used the oil to fry something which has left its taste in the oil, such as seafood, just freshen the oil by frying a slice of lemon and a large cube of bread in it, then reuse.

Baking is not something many people have tried using olive oil for, but it produces a light, fluffy taste and a moist, even texture in breads, rolls, muffins, and cakes. Just substitute olive oil for butter or margarine in a recipe and enjoy the results. And, because of its antioxidants, olive oil will even keep those baked goods fresher longer.

Avoid buying oil in plastic containers because the oil can absorb some of the compounds used in the plastic. However, olive oil is less likely to go rancid than other oils and can be kept for up to two years, longer than any other edible oil, by storing it in a cool cupboard away from light and heat. You may also refrigerate the oil, though this will make it cloudy. The cloudiness will disappear when the oil returns to room temperature.

Here are some other uses for olive oil:

➺ Use a mixture of olive oil and fresh herbs for a bread spread instead of butter or margarine.

➺ Drizzle olive oil and vinegar on your sandwich instead of mayonnaise.

➺ When dining out, ask your waiter for a cruet of olive oil instead of butter.

➺ Pop your popcorn in olive oil, then drizzle extra virgin oil over the top and sprinkle with Parmesan cheese.

➺ Fill a plastic spray-pump bottle with olive oil instead of buying expensive cooking sprays.

➺ Grease pans for baking with olive oil instead of butter or shortening.

➺ When broiling meat, fish, or poultry, brush them with olive oil to seal in the natural juices.

➺ Cut the cholesterol of a recipe by substituting an egg white plus a teaspoon of olive oil for each whole egg.

OLIVE OIL AND HEALTH

Olive oil is a natural storehouse of vitamins A, E, D, and K, and has been shown to have beneficial effects on virtually every aspect of body function, development, and maintenance, including brain development, bone structure, digestive system, aging process, skin condition, hair condition, metabolic balance, and last, but certainly not least, circulatory system. Many of these health benefits have been attributed to olive oil for centuries, since the time of the great physicians of antiquity, including Hippocrates, Galen, Dioscorides, and Diocles.

Throughout ancient times, the people of the Mediterranean used olive oil for promoting the healing of wounds, soothing wind- or sun-damaged skin and aching muscles, making hair shine, curing insomnia, nausea, cholera, and ulcers, as well as preventing wrinkles. Early medical practitioners claimed that olive oil also slowed the aging processes of the brain, internal organs, and tissues.

Today much research supports the claims made so long ago by medical pioneers. The most widely touted scientific finds of late have been the ever-increasing numbers of studies that show the beneficial effects of olive oil on serum cholesterol. Since cholesterol is not soluble in water, it floats through our bodies, attaching itself to proteins, making them lipoproteins. Studies have shown that their are two types of cholesterol: LDL (low-density lipoproteins), the so-called "bad" cholesterol which deposits in bodily tissues and clings to artery walls as plaque, causing arteriosclerosis if unchecked; and HDL (high-density lipoproteins), the "good" cholesterol, which helps prevent artery-clogging deposits. The levels of these two cholesterols are affected by the types of fat we daily ingest.

Saturated, monounsaturated, and polyunsaturated are all terms used to describe the structures of different fats. Saturated fats come primarily from animal meats and tropical oils (palm, palm kernel, and coconut). They are thought to do the greatest damage to our health, because they raise the levels of LDLs, encouraging arteriosclerosis.

Polyunsaturated fats, which come from vegetables, seeds, nuts, and grains, lower the body's general cholesterol level, but reduce both LDLs and HDLs (the bad and the good cholesterols).

Polyunsaturates have been shown in tests to be potentially more damaging than helpful in higher doses, increasing risk of nervous system problems, brain synapse problems, gallstones, and perhaps even cancer, unless their action is checked by antioxidants.

Monounsaturated fats, on the other hand, which are found in varying amounts in all fats, lower LDLs while promoting HDLs. Therefore, the best oil one could use would be one which is low in saturated and polyunsaturated fats, but high in monounsaturated fats. Olive oil has some of the lowest levels of saturated and polyunsaturated fats, averaging 10 percent to 15 percent and 8 percent to 9 percent, respectively. Furthermore, olive oil has by far the highest level of monounsaturated fat of any oil, about 75 percent to 82 percent. For these reasons, olive oil is now thought not only to prevent an increase in cholesterol levels, but also to lower existing levels in the blood.

The unsaponifiable component of olive oil is primarily antioxidants, with tocopherols, primarily alpha-tocopherol, which acts as vitamin E, and betacarotene as provitamin A, as the largest group. Among other things, these antioxidants work to prevent the oxidation of LDLs and highly unsaturated fatty acids, which are essential to nerve-cell functioning. Such oxidation can cause cell and artery damage and lead to arteriosclerosis, coronary heart disease, or possibly, cancer.

Debate about the benefits of antioxidants in cancer prevention continues to rage, but antioxidants are a proven source of vitamin E. Some studies have indicated that diets poor in vitamin E accelerate the peroxidation of certain fatty acids, a process which invariably accompanies aging. Olive oil's vitamin E content is thought to provide a defense against such peroxidative effects, possibly maintaining mental faculties and muscular control better and longer.

As we get older we develop a much more reduced digestive capacity and have more difficulty absorbing nutrients from our food, especially vitamins and mineral salts. Olive oil is very digestible and its nutrients are readily accessible and therefore easier to digest. It also aids digestion and stimulates the appetite.

In addition, another problem associated with aging—bone calcification—seems to be helped by olive oil consumption. In fact, studies have found that a diet adequate in oleates, as well as a moderate supply of essential fatty acids, is necessary for healthy bone mineralization (a process which both aids developing bones in children and prevents calcium loss in adults).

There is no other readily available food that has so much scientific evidence establishing its enviable qualities, nor any that has so many positive effects on so many different parts of the body and their functions than do olives. These health benefits can be derived from all forms of olive oil, except some refined oils which have undergone processes which destroy or alter some of the antioxidants. If you want to make sure you are obtaining the maximum benefit, use only unrefined olive oils.

The early Greeks believed that olive oil had certainly been given to them as a gift from the gods, for the oil nurtured them in lean times and protected them from excess in times of prosperity. The same maxim holds true today.

AN OLIVE OIL GLOSSARY

There are many terms bandied about in discussions of olive oils. In general, they just tend to confuse the consumer unnecessarily. The only two terms you really need to know when purchasing oils are "extra virgin" and "olive oil." Armed with a knowledge of these two terms and your taste buds, you should have no trouble finding an oil you like and can afford. To avoid confusion, however, below is an extensive listing of the most commonly used olive oil terminologies.

Aceite de oliva Spanish for olive oil. Aceite comes from the Arabic for "olive juice."

Cold Pressed The process of pressing olives without any heat or added solvents. Cold-pressed olives should be pressed soon after harvesting. Used mainly by smaller producers today, it is widely thought to produce the best and most flavorful oils, but in small quantities and usually at the highest prices.

Extra Light Like "lite," only more so.

Extra Virgin The cream of the crop. This is a virgin oil with an acidity level of no more than 1 gram per 100 grams of oil. It offers a wide range of aromas and flavors, with perfect taste. Because it is produced in smaller amounts, it generally costs more.

Fine Virgin   A virgin oil with an acidity level of no more than 1.5 grams per 100 grams of oil. These are oils not quite good enough to be called extra virgin.

Fruity   Having a pronounced olive flavor.

Huile d'olive   French for olive oil.

Lampante Virgin   Olive oil which, because of its high acidity level, requires further processing to make it palatable. It would then be blended with virgin oils to be labeled "olive oil."

Lite   The same fat and calories, but less taste.

Mild   Denotes a light, buttery taste.

Olia di oliva   Italian for olive oil.

Olive Oil   A blend of refined oil and virgin oil. Some of the oil that is extracted from olives is done so by the addition of heat or chemical agents, then refining (olive pomace oil), and some is from poorer quality olives with little taste, or from areas where growing conditions were not ideal (lampante virgin oil). These blended oils share the same properties as virgin and extra virgin, but have higher acidity and no taste. They are blended with 5 percent to 25 percent virgin oils to achieve a pleasing flavor.

Olive Pomace Oil   The bottom of the barrel. Pomace is the portion of the olive paste that remains after pressing and centrifuging. More oil can still be removed from it by the addition of heat or solvents which leach the last of the oil from the residue. The term has been in use since 1986, replacing "olive residue oil."

Organoleptic Assessment   This is the numerical rating, from 0 to 9, given olive oils by a panel of 8 to 12 testers who sample the oils under controlled conditions, grading the intensity with which certain attributes of the oil are perceived. Essentially a panel of judges rates the flavor of the oils based on criteria established by the International Olive Oil Council. To date, this is the only method for comparing the olfactory, gustatory, and tactile attributes of oils.

Pizzico   Having a peppery element to its taste.

Pure Olive Oil   If you find a bottle with this on it, it's old. This was the alternative term for "olive oil" blends up until 1990. Some old cookbooks may contain it, however.

Refined Oil   All of the oil with none of the olive. Oil which has been extracted with the use of solvents or heat, then refined to remove those same solvents, as well as the taste, color, and odor. If it is to be used for consumption, it must be blended with virgin oil to acquire some organoleptic qualities.

Robust   Full-flavored and assertive. The term is used by oil tasters to describe an oil's attributes, and by manufacturers to describe their products.

Rustic   Having a full, hearty flavor; too heavy for some people.

Semifruity   Generally mild, but with a distinct, though not over-bearing, olive taste.

Virgin   This is the designation given all oil, extracted by simple pressing of the fruit under controlled thermal and physical conditions that do not cause any deterioration in the attributes of the oil. If sold as is, it is labeled "extra virgin," "fine virgin," or "virgin," depending on its acidity level and organoleptic assessment.

PART TWO

The Recipes

CHAPTER 4

The Appetizing Olive

The Three-Olive Martini

ecipes for martinis are numerous and varied, and aficionados have their favorites. This one is special because it has all the elements that make a martini a delight—it's very dry and uses both gin and vodka as a base. It also uses three olives instead of one. The olives don't have to be pitted or even green. Niçoise are an untraditional but good choice. You may even use three different kinds for a truly special martini.

Preparation time: 5 minutes

Place the ice in a cocktail shaker or pitcher. Pour the vermouth over the ice, swirl briefly, then pour off.

Pour the gin and vodka over the ice. Shake gently.

Then pour the liquid (without the ice) into four martini glasses. Garnish with three olives each, loose or stuck on toothpicks kebab-style, if desired. Serve immediately.

Serves 4

4 cups (1 l) crushed ice

2 tablespoons (30 ml) high quality French or Italian dry vermouth

1 1/4 cups (295 ml) high quality gin

3/4 cup (177 ml) high quality imported vodka

12 small pitted green olives

Retsina Spritzer with Greek Olives

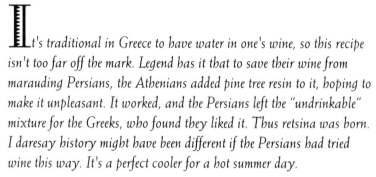

Ice

16 ounces (475 ml) chilled dry white retsina

Seltzer or club soda

4 to 8 Greek black olives, rinsed, dried, and pitted

4 sprigs fresh mint

It's traditional in Greece to have water in one's wine, so this recipe isn't too far off the mark. Legend has it that to save their wine from marauding Persians, the Athenians added pine tree resin to it, hoping to make it unpleasant. It worked, and the Persians left the "undrinkable" mixture for the Greeks, who found they liked it. Thus retsina was born. I daresay history might have been different if the Persians had tried wine this way. It's a perfect cooler for a hot summer day.

Preparation time: 2 minutes

Fill each of four 10- or 12-ounce (300 or 355 ml) glasses with ice. Add 4 ounces (120 ml) of retsina to each and fill with seltzer. Drop 1 or 2 olives and a sprig of mint into each glass and serve.

Serves 4

Pepper Vodka with a
Pepper-Stuffed Olive

A dazzling combination of cold and hot, but not for the faint-hearted. This cocktail will take the roof off your mouth, but warm you to your lowest cockles. The pepper-stuffed olive is there to give an added kick. You may use the ones in cans at your local supermarket or specialty store, or make them yourself by stuffing a piece of a hot pepper into a pitted Manzanilla olive. There are several brands of imported vodka flavored with hot peppers on the market today. Ouch, it hurts so good!

Preparation time: 2 minutes, plus time for chilling vodka

Pour 2 ounces (50 ml) vodka in each of 4 small glasses. Drop an olive into each. Add ice if desired (or not, if you think you can take the heat). Serve immediately, but not without warning.

Serves 4

8 ounces (200 ml) imported pepper-flavored vodka, chilled in the freezer

4 hot pepper-stuffed green olives

Ice (optional)

Spicy California Sicilian-Style Olives

1 1/2 pounds (675 g) California Sicilian-style olives, drained and rinsed

3 strips lemon zest, about 3/4 inches by 2 1/2 inches (1.9 by 6.35 cm), removed with a vegetable peeler

3 cloves garlic, whacked and peeled

2 teaspoons (10 ml) dried thyme

2 teaspoons (10 ml) dried oregano

1 tablespoon (15 ml) crushed red pepper flakes

2 medium-sized bay leaves, broken up

1 teaspoon (5 ml) celery seeds

1 teaspoon (5 ml) freshly ground black pepper

Extra virgin olive oil to cover

Sprigs of fresh thyme and oregano for garnish (optional)

Any brine-cured olive can be improved by removing it from it's brine, rinsing it, and dressing it with flavorful herbs and olive oil. This spicy version is ready to be eaten in about a week. You are actually making two condiments here, spicy olives and a flavorful oil you can use when the olives are gone. You may substitute any brine-cured green olive or alter the pepper flakes to your taste.

Preparation time: 10 minutes, plus 7 to 10 days marinating time

Cover the bottom of a 1-quart (*1 l*) jar with a layer of olives, a piece of lemon peel, and a garlic clove.

In a small bowl combine the thyme, oregano, pepper flakes, bay leaves, celery seeds, and black pepper. Sprinkle some of the mixture over the olives in the jar.

Continue to alternate layers of olives and herbs, interspersing the remaining lemon peel and garlic cloves, until the jar is full and the herbs are all used. Fill the jar to cover with olive oil. Allow to sit at room temperature 7 to 10 days before serving. Garnish with sprigs of fresh herbs, if desired.

If storing longer, remove garlic cloves after 10 days to 2 weeks and store up to 6 months in the refrigerator. Allow to return to room temperature before serving. When the olives have been used, strain oil, return to room temperature, and use for salad dressings, drizzling on vegetables or bruschetta, or basting grilled foods.

Makes I Quart (I L)

Caponata

1 medium-sized eggplant, about 1 1/2 pounds (675 g)

2 teaspoons (10 ml) salt

3 tablespoons (45 ml) olive oil

1 medium-sized onion, chopped

2 ribs celery, chopped

2 medium-sized tomatoes, peeled and chopped

2 tablespoons (30 ml) capers, rinsed and drained, chopped if large

1/2 cup (118 ml) chopped, pitted green olives

3 tablespoons (45 ml) red wine vinegar

1 tablespoon (15 ml) firmly packed, dark brown sugar

3 tablespoons (45 ml) tomato paste

1 tablespoon (15 ml) chopped fresh parsley leaves

Salt and freshly ground black pepper, to taste

2 tablespoons (30 ml) extra virgin olive oil

A sweet-and-sour eggplant salad, originally of Sicilian or southern Italian origin, caponata makes a wonderful addition to an antipasto plate; a luscious spread for bruschetta, crackers, or sandwiches; or a delicious relish for roasted meats and poultry. This recipe should serve six to eight, but I once served it with crackers to three people who were so taken by it they scraped the bowl clean! You may use any brine-cured green olive in it. (I use Manzanilla because they're available already pitted.) If you use white eggplant, you can skip the initial salting and draining. You'll have to try both the original and the Sicilian variation to see which you like better. They're both heavenly—the best use for eggplant ever!

Preparation time: 45 minutes, plus 1 hour draining and at least 1 hour cooling time

Peel the eggplant and cut into 3/4-inch (2 cm) cubes. Place the cubes in a colander and sprinkle with the 2 teaspoons (10 ml) of salt. Place a plate or bowl on top with a couple of pounds of weight on it (bagged rice or canned goods work well). Leave the colander in the sink to drain for one hour.

Rinse, then pat the eggplant dry between paper towels. Heat 2 tablespoons (30 ml) of the oil in a large nonreactive skillet over medium-high heat and fry the eggplant until lightly browned, about 12 minutes. Remove to a small bowl and reserve.

Put the last tablespoon of oil in the skillet and add the onion and celery. Sauté 3 to 4 minutes until the onion is soft and translucent. Add the tomatoes to the pan, cover, lower the heat, and simmer 15 minutes, stirring occasionally.

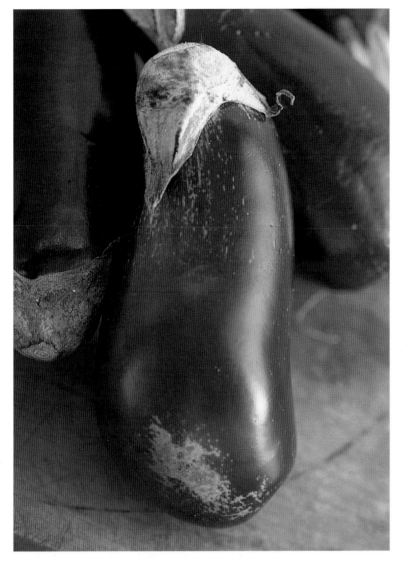

SICILIAN VARIATION:
Lightly brown ¹/₂ cup (118 ml) pine nuts in the oil before cooking the eggplant. Drain on paper towels. Add ¹/₄ cup (59 ml) golden raisins with the capers and olives. Add the pine nuts when cooled.

Uncover the pan, add the eggplant and the remaining ingredients, except the extra virgin oil, and simmer uncovered 5 minutes or until thickened. Remove from the heat and cool to room temperature. When cooled, stir in the extra virgin oil and serve.

Serves 6 to 8

Marinated Mixed Vegetables with Black and Green Olives

Generous 1/2 cup (118 ml) small-variety, brine-cured black olives

Generous 1/2 cup (118 ml) small-variety, brine-cured green olives

10 to 12 small cauliflower florets

10 to 14 pearl onions, unpeeled

1/2 cup (118 ml) baby carrots

1 thin cucumber, cut into 5 or 6 1-inch (2.5 cm) lengths

4 small garlic cloves, unpeeled

1 small red pepper, quartered and seeded

10 to 12 button mushrooms

1 stalk celery, cut into 1 1/2-inch (3.5 cm) lengths

2 cups (472 ml) white wine vinegar

1/2 cup (118 ml) water

1 1/2 tablespoons (22.5 ml) salt

2 tablespoons (30 ml) sugar

1 tablespoon (15 ml) yellow mustard seeds

2 whole cloves

1 dried red chili pepper

6 black peppercorns

2 sprigs fresh tarragon, rosemary

Extra virgin olive oil to cover

You often see these beautiful vegetables layered in large jars in fine food stores and charcuteries. This recipe makes a slightly more modest quantity, and you may layer or arrange them in the jar to your liking or just put them in at random. Either way, they're lovely as a gift or as part of an antipasto tray or picnic. You may freely substitute vegetables, olives, or fresh herbs of your choice, but keep in mind the size of your jar and how much of each ingredient it will take to make a layer.

Preparation time: 25 minutes, plus 24 hours in vinegar and 2 weeks marinating time

Bring a 4-quart (3.8 *l*) pot of water to a boil. Add the olives and vegetables and blanch for 4 minutes after the water returns to a boil. Drain in a colander. Take out the onions and the garlic cloves and drop them in a small bowl of cold water until cool enough to handle. Put the rest of the vegetables into a 2-quart (1.8 *l*) glass or ceramic bowl.

In a small pan, bring the vinegar to a boil. While it heats, peel the onions and garlic by cutting off a tiny bit of the root end, splitting the outer skin, and removing it. Add the onions and garlic to the rest of the vegetables, pour the boiling vinegar over them, cover, and let sit overnight.

The following day, drain the vinegar off into a pot. Add the remaining ingredients to the pot, except the fresh herb sprigs and olive oil, and bring to a boil. Reduce heat and simmer gently for 5 minutes.

Meanwhile, put the fresh herb sprigs and vegetables into a 34-ounce (1 *l*) jar, randomly, or arranged in layers or designs. (If layering, use garlic cloves and any excess pieces to fill in the center where needed.) Pour the vinegar over the vegetables to within 1/2 inch (1 *cm*) of the top of the jar. Pour a 1/8 inch (.5 *cm*) layer of olive oil on top. Seal and let marinate 2 weeks before serving. Refrigerate after opening.

If not to be used within 3 to 4 weeks, process 10 minutes in a boiling-water bath.

Makes I quart (IL)

Garlic Shrimp with Atalanta Olives

4 tablespoons (60 ml) olive oil

3 cloves garlic, minced

1 1/2 pounds (675 g)
fresh medium shrimp, peeled
and deveined

1/4 cup (59 ml) dry white wine

2 tablespoons (30 ml) freshly
squeezed lime juice

1/4 teaspoon (1.25 ml) cayenne
pepper, or to taste

1 cup (236 ml) pitted
Atalanta olives

2 tablespoons (30 ml) finely
chopped fresh coriander leaves

I*nspired by traditional Greek and Caribbean cuisines, these tasty shrimp can be served in a bowl with toothpicks as an hors d'oeuvre, in a small portion on a plate of lettuce as a starter, or in a larger portion on greens as an entrée. Other full-flavored olives, such as Alphonso, Gaeta, Kalamata, Naphlion, or Niçoise, may be substituted, but you'll have to pit them yourself. Atalantas are usually sold pitted.*

Preparation time: 25 minutes

Heat the oil in a large, nonreactive skillet over medium-high heat. Add the garlic and sauté 15 seconds. Add the shrimp and sauté, tossing to coat with the oil and garlic, for 1 minute. Add the wine, lime juice, and cayenne pepper. Raise heat and cook, stirring constantly, until the liquid is reduced to a syrup and the shrimp are uniformly pink.

Remove from the heat, add the olives and coriander, and toss well to combine. Serve hot or at room temperature, with toothpicks or on lettuce leaves.

Serves 4 to 6 as an entrée, 6 to 8 as a starter or hors d'oeuvre

Chinese Preserved Olives Steamed with Ginger

Olives preserved with salt, sugar, and licorice root are available in Chinese grocery stores in plastic bags and clear plastic boxes. (They also sell salted olives, but they're harder to find and not what we want for this recipe.) Preserved olives are sweet and salty and are eaten right out of the bag like candy in China, but steaming tenderizes them. The addition of ginger makes them even better. Serve these along with dessert or as part of an hors d'oeuvre assortment. This is truly one of the most unusual treatments of olives you'll find anywhere. Delicious, but so full of flavor you can't eat huge quantities, and possibly, too unusual for the nonadventurous.

Preparation time: 15 minutes

Toss the olives with the ginger, coating them as thoroughly and evenly as possible, or wipe the ginger on each one with your fingers. Place them on a rack over simmering water, cover, and steam about 10 minutes, or until tender.

Transfer the olives to a bowl. Serve warm.

Serves 6

1 cup (236 ml) Chinese preserved olives

4 teaspoons (20 ml) grated fresh ginger root

Bruschetta with Latium Oil

6 thick slices crusty,
country-style bread

2 cloves garlic, peeled and halved

4 to 6 tablespoons (60 to 90 ml)
good quality olive oil from
Latium (Lazio)

Salt and freshly ground black
pepper to taste

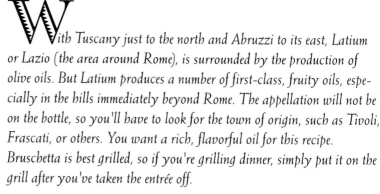

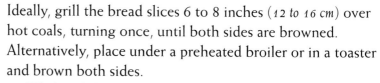

With Tuscany just to the north and Abruzzi to its east, Latium or Lazio (the area around Rome), is surrounded by the production of olive oils. But Latium produces a number of first-class, fruity oils, especially in the hills immediately beyond Rome. The appellation will not be on the bottle, so you'll have to look for the town of origin, such as Tivoli, Frascati, or others. You want a rich, flavorful oil for this recipe. Bruschetta is best grilled, so if you're grilling dinner, simply put it on the grill after you've taken the entrée off.

Preparation time: 5 minutes

Ideally, grill the bread slices 6 to 8 inches (12 to 16 cm) over hot coals, turning once, until both sides are browned. Alternatively, place under a preheated broiler or in a toaster and brown both sides.

While still hot, rub one side of each slice with the cut side of the garlic. The garlic will disintegrate. Drizzle oil over each slice and sprinkle with salt and pepper.

Serve immediately as is, or sprinkle with oregano, or together with a tapenade.

Serves 4 to 6

Black Olive and Tomato Tapenade

Tapenades are very rich pastes of olives, capers, anchovies, and olive oil. Anchovy haters needn't worry, though, because the anchovy taste here becomes a part of the whole. You can use any black olives you want—Nyons and Kalamatas are very good. This tapenade is also one of the best ways to spice up relatively bland, canned California ripe olives, and they're already pitted! Use the tapenade on bruschetta or crackers, or as you would salsa or a crudite dip.

Preparation time: 15 minutes

Combine all ingredients, except the tomato and coriander, in a blender or food processor. Process, pulsing on and off and scraping down the sides of the container as needed, until smooth and well combined. By hand, stir in the tomato.

If making ahead, refrigerate covered, then return to room temperature. Serve garnished with coriander or parsley, if desired.

Serves 6 to 8

1 1/2 cups (354 ml) pitted California ripe olives, drained

2 tablespoons (30 ml) capers, rinsed and drained

2 anchovy fillets, rinsed and patted dry

2 cloves garlic, whacked and peeled

2 tablespoons (30 ml) chopped onion

1 1/2 teaspoons (7.5 ml) fresh oregano leaves (or 1/2 teaspoon, 2.5 ml, dried)

2 teaspoons (10 ml) Dijon mustard

1/4 cup (59 ml) extra virgin olive oil

1 medium-sized tomato, peeled, seeded, and chopped

1 tablespoon (15 ml) finely chopped fresh coriander or parsley leaves (optional)

Dressed Olives
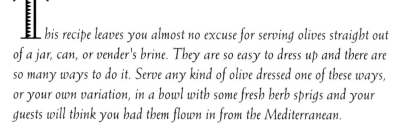

2 cups (472 ml) olives,
rinsed and drained

1/4 cup (59 ml)
extra virgin olive oil

2 tablespoons (30 ml)
red wine vinegar

2 garlic cloves,
peeled and thinly sliced

*T*his recipe leaves you almost no excuse for serving olives straight out of a jar, can, or vender's brine. They are so easy to dress up and there are so many ways to do it. Serve any kind of olive dressed one of these ways, or your own variation, in a bowl with some fresh herb sprigs and your guests will think you had them flown in from the Mediterranean.

Preparation time: 5 minutes, plus marinating time

Whisk together oil and vinegar. Toss all ingredients together in bowl. Let marinate at room temperature from 4 hours to overnight.

VARIATIONS:

Add 1 fresh hot chili pepper, seeded and chopped (or 1/2 teaspoon, 2.5 ml, crushed red pepper flakes).

Add the zest of a lemon, removed with a vegetable peeler and cut into strips.

Add the zest of an orange removed with a vegetable peeler and cut into strips and 1 teaspoon (5 ml) fennel seeds, lightly crushed.

Add 1 tablespoon (15 ml) finely chopped fresh herb leaves (or 1 teaspoon, 5 ml, dried).

Add 1/4 cup (59 ml) drained and rinsed capers and 1/2 teaspoon (2.5 ml) freshly ground black pepper.

Add 1 tablespoon (15 ml) chili powder and 1 teaspoon (5 ml) cayenne pepper.

Serves 6 to 8

Leeks with Mozzarella and Kalamata Olives

There has been a tendency to use leeks as a flavoring rather than as the vegetables they are. But as the mildest member of the onion family, I think they deserve more of a starring role. They get top billing in this dish, nestled with tart Kalamatas under a creamy blanket of bubbling mozzarella. You may substitute any of the less bitter, brine-cured black olives.

Preparation time: 55 minutes

Trim the dark green tops from the leeks, leaving the pale green and white parts. Discard the tops or save for broth. Trim off the roots and slice each leek in half lengthwise. Remove the outer leaves if they're tough or darkened. Wash the leek halves under running water, pulling the leaves apart and rinsing both sides of each. Rub off dirt with your fingers. Drain. Slice into 1-inch (2.5 cm) lengths. Cut off enough of the root end that the leaves aren't held together.

Preheat the oven to 375°F (190°C). Oil a shallow, 2-quart (1.9 l), nonreactive baking dish or gratin pan and set it aside.

Heat the oil in a large, nonreactive skillet over medium heat. Add the leeks and garlic. Sauté until the leeks are bright green and slightly limp, 3 to 5 minutes. Add the red wine, allspice, vinegar, olives, basil, and pepper, and mix well.

Spoon the leeks into the casserole and spread the cheese over them. Sprinkle with nutmeg and bake in preheated oven 20 to 25 minutes until the cheese is lightly browned and bubbly. Serve immediately.

Serves 6

6 to 8 medium-sized fresh leeks (about 3 pounds, or 454 g, before trimming)

1/4 cup (59 ml) olive oil

1 clove garlic, minced

1/2 cup (118 ml) dry red wine

1/4 teaspoon (1.25 ml) ground allspice

2 teaspoons (10 ml) balsamic vinegar

1 cup (236 ml) sliced, pitted Kalamata olives

2 tablespoons (30 ml) chopped fresh basil leaves (or 2 teaspoons, 10 ml, dried)

Freshly ground black pepper to taste

10 ounces (280 g) mozzarella cheese, shredded

Generous pinch freshly grated nutmeg

CHAPTER 5

The Well-Seasoned Olive

Mixed Nut and California Sicilian-Style Olive Spread

This incredibly rich spread can be made a day ahead and refrigerated. Remember to take it out in advance so that it can warm up to a spreadable consistency. Wonderful as an hors d'oeuvre, it's equally good as a sandwich, spread on whole-grain bread. You may substitute other brine-cured green olives.

Preparation time: 25 minutes

Preheat oven to 350°F (177°C).

Place almonds in an 8-inch (18 cm) cake or pie pan and roast in the preheated oven for 10 minutes. Add the hazelnuts, pecans, and pine nuts to the pan, spreading them out to a single layer, and continue to roast 5 to 7 minutes more, until the pine nuts are golden brown.

Remove the nuts from the pan and cool completely. Finely chop by hand or in a food processor.

In a mixing bowl, stir together the two cheeses and the cream, mixing well. Add the parsley, pepper, olives, and chopped nuts and combine thoroughly. Place in a serving bowl and smooth or sculpt as desired. May be covered and refrigerated several hours or overnight. Remove one hour before serving to soften.

Serves 6 to 8

1/4 cup (59 ml) blanched whole almonds

1/4 cup (59 ml) peeled hazelnuts

1/4 cup (59 ml) pecan halves

1/4 cup (59 ml) pine nuts

51/2 ounce (155 g) log Montrachet, or other mild chevre, at room temperature

8 ounces (225 g) Neufchatel or cream cheese, at room temperature

2 tablespoons (30 ml) heavy cream

2 tablespoons (30 ml) finely chopped fresh parsley leaves

1/4 teaspoon (1.25 ml) freshly ground black pepper, or to taste

1/2 cup (118 ml) pitted and chopped California Sicilian-style olives

Moroccan Olive Spread

1 cup (236 ml) pitted Moroccan oil-cured olives

1/2 cup (118 ml) extra virgin olive oil, plus extra to cover top

1 tablespoon (15 ml) ground cumin

2 teaspoons (10 ml) ground coriander

1 teaspoon (5 ml) cayenne pepper

1 teaspoon (5 ml) caraway seeds

2 cloves garlic, whacked and peeled

Here's a caviar look-alike that will wake up just about any food. This spicy concoction is great spread on bruschetta or crackers, sandwiches, or thick beefsteak tomato slices. It can be stirred into couscous, rice or bean dishes, or used as a condiment. Inspired by the harissa-dressed olives available in Moroccan markets, any oil-cured or roasted olives can be used, but the moister ones are easier to tear apart and pit.

Preparation time: 15 minutes

Place all ingredients in a blender or food processor. Purée the mixture, pausing to scrape down the sides as needed, until an evenly chopped rough paste is formed. If too dry, drizzle a little more oil into it. The result should look like black caviar.

Use immediately, or store up to 2 weeks in the refrigerator, covered with a thin layer of olive oil. Return to room temperature before using.

Makes about 1 1/4 cups (295 ml)

Olive and Herb Butter

Here's a delightful way to make a baguette or loaf of Italian bread special. Serve this flavored butter in place of the usual stick. It can be presented in ramekins, sliced on bread plates, or even in butter molds if you have them. It's also great in place of mayonnaise on a roast beef sandwich, or served on plain rice or noodles. Feel free to use any type of green olive and whatever and however many types of fresh herbs you wish.

Preparation time: 10 minutes, plus time for softening and chilling butter

8 ounces (1 stick, 225 g) unsalted butter, at room temperature

1/4 cup (59 ml) finely chopped green olives

2 tablespoons (30 ml) finely chopped fresh herb leaves

In a small bowl, stir the butter with the olives and herbs until well blended. Spoon into ramekins or butter molds, smooth tops, and refrigerate, or spoon into the center of a 10-inch (25 cm) piece of wax paper and form loosely into the shape of a stick of butter.

Fold the wax paper over the butter mixture and place a pencil or wooden dowel on top of the waxed paper where it meets. Holding the edges of the paper, push the pencil against the butter, causing the paper to tighten and the butter to become more even and cylindrical. Remove the pencil and roll up the butter in the paper. Place the roll on a smooth, flat surface in the refrigerator for 20 minutes or so, until it begins to get firm. Twist the ends of the wax paper to seal the roll and leave refrigerated from 2 hours to overnight to get completely firm.

At serving time, remove wax paper and slice 1/4-inch (75 cm) thick. Re-wrap unused portion and keep refrigerated. Will keep in refrigerator 2 weeks.

Serves 6 to 8

Smoked Salmon Rolls with Olive Cream Cheese

1/3 cup (79 ml) chopped, pitted, brine-cured green olives

8 ounces (225 g) cream cheese, softened

2 tablespoons (30 g) freshly squeezed lemon juice

2 tablespoons (30 g) finely chopped fresh chives

1/4 teaspoon (1.25 ml) freshly ground black pepper, or to taste

8 ounces (225 g) thinly sliced smoked salmon

Whole chives (optional)

An attractive addition to an hors d'oeuvre table, these salmon rolls look as if they were more work than they really were. I prefer nova to lox for these, simply because it's less salty, but either is okay. Tying each roll with a chive looks pretty, but they will hold together without any assistance.

Preparation time: 20 minutes

In a small mixing bowl, thoroughly combine the chopped olives with the cream cheese, lemon juice, chopped chives, and pepper. Taste and adjust seasoning as needed.

Place a thin slice of salmon on the counter or board, with one of the narrow ends toward you. Place a rounded tablespoon of the olive mixture on the end nearest you and roll up in the salmon. Carefully tie a whole chive around the roll and trim ends, if desired.

Repeat with remaining salmon and cheese, arrange on a serving plate, cover tightly with plastic wrap, and refrigerate until serving time.

Serves 6 to 8

Olive Oil Mayonnaises

BASIC MAYONNAISE:

1 large egg yolk

1 teaspoon (5 ml) Dijon mustard
or dry mustard

1 cup (236 ml) olive oil

Salt to taste

Pinch cayenne pepper

1 to 2 tablespoons (15 to 30 ml)
freshly squeezed lemon juice
or vinegar

1 or 2 tablespoons (15 or 30 ml)
hot water

If you've never made your own, homemade mayonnaise is well worth the effort. Without the preservatives that give commercial mayonnaise a shelf life of numerous years, homemade only lasts four to five days, so it's best to make it for specific uses and in small quantities. If you're making a basic mayonnaise, you may want to experiment with different flavors of olive oil and different kinds of vinegars.

Preparation time: 5 minutes

In a mixing bowl (if you're mixing by hand), the bowl of an electric mixer, blender, or food processor, place the egg yolk, mustard, and a couple of tablespoons of oil and whisk or beat them until pale yellow.

Add the remaining oil a few drops at a time at first, while whisking or with machine running, then in a steady, thin stream. Once the mixture starts to thicken, you may add the oil slightly faster, until all of it is incorporated. Scrape down sides of the bowl, add the salt, cayenne, and lemon juice and beat in briefly. Taste and adjust seasoning. If the mayonnaise is too thick, beat in a tablespoon (*15 ml*) or so of hot tap water. Transfer to a clean container, seal and store in refrigerator up to 5 days.

Note: If the mixture separates or curdles, get a new bowl, and egg yolk and beat in the old mixture. Or pour all but 1 tablespoon (*15 ml*) out of the bowl you're using. Add 1 tablespoon (*15 ml*) of water to the tablespoon (*15 ml*) of failed mixture and whisk or beat. Continue to whisk or beat, while adding the rest of the separated mayonnaise gradually.

Makes approximately 1 cup (236 ml)

VARIATIONS:

≪AïOLI~Add second egg yolk and 5 cloves garlic, minced.

≪CAPER~Add 3 tablespoons (45 ml) ketchup and 2 tablespoons (30 ml) minced capers.

≪CAVIAR~Add 2 tablespoons (30 ml) caviar and 1 tablespoon (15 ml) chopped chives.

≪CUCUMBER~Add one large cucumber, peeled, seeded, thinly sliced, mixed with 1 teaspoon (5 ml) salt in a colander for 30 minutes, squeezed dry of excess water, and chopped fine, plus 1 teaspoon (5 ml) sugar.

≪DIJONNAISE~Add 1 tablespoon (15 ml) more Dijon mustard.

≪DILL~Add 1/4 cup (59 ml) finely chopped dill.

≪HORSERADISH~Add 2 tablespoons (30 ml) grated fresh or prepared horseradish, 1 tablespoon (15 ml) finely chopped dill, and 1 teaspoon (5 ml) grated lemon zest.

≪OLIVE~Add 2 tablespoons (30 ml) olive paste or tapenade.

≪PESTO~Add 2 tablespoons (30 ml) prepared pesto.

≪REMOULADE~Add 2 more teaspoons (10 ml) Dijon, 1 anchovy fillet, rinsed and patted dry (or 1/2 teaspoon (2.5 ml) anchovy paste), 1 tablespoon (15 ml) chopped sweet pickles, 1 tablespoon (15 ml) chopped capers, 1 tablespoon (15 ml) finely chopped parsley.

≪RICH~Use 2 egg yolks instead of one.

≪SESAME~Use rice vinegar and 1 tablespoon (15 ml) soy sauce instead of lemon juice and salt, and add 3 tablespoons (45 ml) sesame oil.

≪SPICY~Use lime juice instead of lemon juice or vinegar, add 1/4 cup (59 ml) finely chopped coriander or parsley, 1 clove minced garlic, and 2 hot peppers, seeded and chopped.

≪TARRAGON~Add 1 tablespoon (15 ml) finely chopped fresh tarragon.

Olive Oil Marinades

BASIC MARINADE:

²/₃ cup (157 ml) olive oil

3 tablespoons (45 ml) vinegar or
citrus juice

1 clove garlic, whacked and
peeled

Freshly ground black pepper,
to taste

Olive oil makes wonderful marinades for beef, lamb, veal, pork, chicken, turkey, game, fish, seafood, vegetables—just about anything you can cook. When exposed to heat, it helps seal the food, trapping the moisture inside for juicier results. Marinades have long been used to shorten cooking times by as much as a third, to make less expensive cuts of meat more tender, and less fresh purchases more palatable. The length of time the food should stay in the marinade depends on what it is and how big it is, from an hour or so for a fish fillet, to two or three days for a beef roast. Dry the food before marinating and make sure previously frozen foods are completely thawed. Use a nonreactive container and turn the food in the marinade regularly to insure even flavoring. Marinating for up to an hour can be done at room temperature, but longer should be done in the refrigerator. Always cover tightly and never add salt until cooking!

Mix all ingredients by hand or in a blender and pour over food. Cover tightly and marinate at room temperature or in refrigerator. This makes enough for 1 pound (454 g) of meat, poultry, or fish, except with variations otherwise noted.

VARIATIONS:

✒ BOURBON AND MOLASSES~Use red wine vinegar, lemon, or orange juice. Add 2 tablespoons (30 ml) prepared mustard, 1/2 cup (79 ml) bourbon, 2 tablespoons (30 ml) molasses, and 2 teaspoons (10 ml) Worcestershire sauce. Good for beef, pork, or chicken.

✒ GINGER~Use lemon juice or rice vinegar. Add 2 tablespoons (30 ml) soy sauce, 2 tablespoons (30 ml) dry sherry, and 2 tablespoons (30 ml) freshly grated ginger root. Good for beef, pork, fish, or poultry.

✒ HOT PEPPER~Use red wine vinegar or lime juice. Add 1 teaspoon (5 ml) dry mustard, 1 1/2 teaspoons (7.5 ml) chopped fresh (or 1/2 teaspoon, 2.5 ml, dried) marjoram, and 3 fresh hot peppers, seeded and chopped (or 2 to 3 teaspoons, 10 to 15 ml, red pepper flakes). Good for beef, lamb, pork, chicken, or vegetables.

✒ MEXICAN~Use lime juice. Add 1/4 cup (59 ml) tomato sauce or ketchup, 1 teaspoon (5 ml) paprika, 1 teaspoon (5 ml) ground cumin, 1 tablespoon (15 ml) chopped fresh (or 1 teaspoon, 5 ml, dried) oregano, and 1/2 teaspoon (2.5 ml) cayenne pepper, or to taste. Good for beef, pork, or chicken.

✒ ORANGE AND ROSEMARY~Use 1/2 cup (118 ml) orange juice instead of vinegar. Add 1 tablespoon (15 ml) grated orange zest, and 3 tablespoons (45 ml) chopped fresh (or 1 tablespoon, 15 ml, crushed dried) rosemary. Good for pork or poultry.

✒ RED WINE~Use red wine vinegar. Add 1 cup (236 ml) dry red wine, 1 small onion, sliced, 1 bay leaf, and 1 1/2 teaspoons (7.5 ml) chopped fresh (or 1/2 teaspoon, 2.5 ml, dried) thyme. Good for beef or lamb. Enough for 2 pounds (908 g).

✒ SESAME~Use lemon juice instead of vinegar. Add 1 tablespoon (15 ml) soy sauce, 2 teaspoons (10 ml) sugar, and 2 tablespoons (30 ml) toasted sesame seeds. Good for fish, vegetables, poultry, or meat.

✒ WHITE WINE~Use white wine vinegar or lemon juice. Add 1 cup (236 ml) dry white wine, 1 1/2 teaspoons (7.5 ml) chopped fresh (or 1/2 teaspoon, 2.5 ml, dried) rosemary, and 1 1/2 teaspoon (7.5 ml) chopped fresh (or 1/2 teaspoon, 2.5 ml, dried) thyme. Good for lamb, poultry vegetables, or fish. Enough for 2 pounds (908 g).

✒ YOGURT~Add 2/3 cup (158 ml) plain yogurt, 1 small onion, thinly sliced, 1 tablespoon (15 ml) chopped fresh (or 1 teaspoon, 5 ml, dried) oregano, and 1/2 teaspoon (2.5 ml) cinnamon. Good for beef, lamb, or chicken.

Extra Virgin Vinaigrettes

BASIC VINAIGRETTE:

2/3 cup (157 ml) extra virgin olive oil

1/3 cup (79 ml) wine vinegar

1/4 teaspoon (1.25 ml) salt

1/4 teaspoon (1.25 ml) freshly ground black pepper

*V*inaigrettes are one of the best uses for extra virgin oil. Here their tastes can truly be appreciated. But they aren't just for salads. Use them on steamed vegetables or for basting grilled foods—they make great marinades, too. The possibilities are endless with differently flavored oils and a myriad of things to add. I use a two-to-one oil-to-vinegar ratio, some people prefer a milder three-to one-ratio. Suit yourself.

Place all ingredients in a small jar. Shake well. Alternatively, place the ingredients in a small bowl and whisk until an emulsified blend is achieved. Leftovers can be kept in the tightly closed jar at room temperature for several days.

Makes I cup

VARIATIONS:

≪BLUE CHEESE~Add ¹/₄ cup (59 ml) crumbled blue, Roquefort, or Gorgonzola cheese and 2 tablespoons (30 ml) heavy cream (optional).

≪CAPER~Add 3 tablespoons (45 ml) rinsed and drained small capers and 1 teaspoon (5 ml) sugar.

≪CURRY~Add 1 tablespoon (15 ml) minced shallots and 1 teaspoon curry powder.

≪GARLIC~Add 1 clove garlic, minced and mashed to a paste with the salt.

≪GREEK~Add 1 tablespoon (15 ml) chopped fresh oregano (or 1 teaspoon, 5 ml, dried) and 1 tablespoon (15 ml) chopped fresh parsley to Lemon Vinaigrette.

≪HERB~Add 2 tablespoons (30 ml) finely chopped leaves of one or more herbs (or 2 teaspoons, 10 ml, dried), 1 teaspoon (5 ml) Dijon mustard, and one tablespoon (15 ml) minced shallots.

≪HORSERADISH~Add 2 tablespoons (30 ml) prepared horseradish. Great for seafood salads.

≪JAPANESE~Use rice vinegar. Add 1 tablespoon (15 ml) sugar, 2 teaspoons (10 ml) soy sauce, and 1 teaspoon (5 ml) sesame oil.

≪LEMON~Use freshly squeezed lemon juice instead of the vinegar. Add 1 tablespoon (15 ml) grated lemon zest and 1 teaspoon (5 ml) dry mustard.

≪MUSTARD~Add 2 tablespoons (30 ml) prepared mustard of your choice.

≪SPICY~Add 2 teaspoons (10 ml) chopped fresh oregano (or ³/₄ teaspoon, 3.75 ml, dried), 1 teaspoon (5 ml) ground cumin, and ¹/₂ teaspoon (2.5 ml) red pepper flakes, or to taste, to Garlic Vinaigrette.

≪STELLA'S~Use white-wine tarragon vinegar. Add ¹/₂ teaspoon (2.5 ml) rubbed dried sage, ¹/₂ teaspoon (2.5 ml) dried thyme, 1 teaspoon (5 ml) Dijon mustard, 1 teaspoon (5 ml) sugar, and 1 teaspoon (2.5 ml) soy sauce.

Flavored Olive Oils

Ιn the last couple of years more and more flavored oils have come onto the market. They're quite expensive, though, and it's easy to make your own. These oils are great for using in salad dressings or marinades, for brushing on food to be grilled or drizzling on vegetables, for spicing up pasta or sauces, or just setting in a cruet on the table—in fact, any way you would use regular olive oil.

After two weeks you should always strain the oil to remove the additives—there's a chance of some of them getting moldy and by then the flavors should have been transferred anyway. If you like having a sprig of herb or whatever else you're using in the bottle on the table, use the oil before the two weeks are up or put a new one in it the day you're using it.

Because their flavors are best fresh, make the oils in small quantities, one to two cups (.24 to .48 liters) at a time. Use either extra virgin or less expensive oils, depending on how you're going to use the oil and how strong a flavoring you're using.

To each cup of olive oil in a clean, sealable container, add one or more of the following ingredients, thoroughly washed and dried. Let steep in the oil for two weeks, then strain and remove additive.

Makes I cup

GARLIC OIL~6 peeled, whole, unblemished cloves of garlic, halved and soaked in vinegar for 24 hours.

GINGER OIL~A peeled piece of ginger about 1 1/2-inches (3.81 cm) cubed, thinly sliced.

HERB OILS~3 to 5 fresh sprigs of one or more herbs, lightly bruised with the back of a spoon or the bottom of a glass.

HORSERADISH OIL~A peeled piece of fresh horseradish, 1 1/2-inches (3.81 cm) in diameter by 2-inches (5 cm) long, thinly sliced.

HOT PEPPER OIL~8 to 10 fresh or dried hot peppers, slit with the tip of a sharp knife.

LEMON OIL~The zest of a lemon, removed in long strips with a vegetable peeler or zester. This oil may get cloudy after a few days, but the taste won't be affected.

CHAPTER 6

The Saucy Olive

Chicken Fricassee with Herbs and Moroccan Green Olives

Recipes for chicken with olives abound in the Mediterranean, particularly in North Africa and the Middle East. This is a relatively easy one that's quite delicious. I remove the chicken's skin because I don't think the skin fares well in braised dishes, and it makes the dish healthier. If you wish to remove it, grasp it with a piece of paper towel and it won't slip out of your fingers. You may also alter the herbs to your taste and substitute cracked Provençal or other milder green olives.

Preparation time: 1 hour 35 minutes

Heat oil in a large skillet over medium-high heat. Dredge the chicken pieces in 1/3 cup (*79 ml*) flour to coat, and brown on all sides. Remove to a plate and reserve.

Fry the onions in the oil until they begin to brown. Add the broth, herbs, salt and pepper, and reserved chicken. Bring to a boil, lower heat, cover, and simmer 1 hour, until the chicken is tender.

Combine the remaining tablespoon (*15 ml*) of flour with the cream. Mix in several spoonfuls of the hot broth, then add the mixture to the pan, stirring in well. Add the olives and heat gently, uncovered for 5 to 10 minutes, until the sauce is thickened.

Transfer to a serving dish or individual plates. Garnish with parsley. Serve with rice or mashed potatoes, if desired.

Serves 4

1/3 cup (79 ml) olive oil

1 3 to 4 pound (135 to 180 g) chicken, cut up and skinned

1/3 cup plus 1 tablespoon (79 ml plus 15 ml) unbleached, all-purpose flour

2 cups (472 ml) chopped onion

1 1/2 cups (354 ml) chicken broth

1 tablespoon (15 ml) chopped fresh marjoram leaves (or 1 teaspoon, 5 ml, dried)

1 tablespoon (15 ml) chopped fresh mint leaves (or 1 teaspoon, 5 ml, dried)

1 tablespoon (15 ml) chopped fresh tarragon leaves (or 1 teaspoon, 5 ml, dried)

Salt and freshly ground pepper, to taste

1/2 cup (118 ml) light cream or half-and-half

1 cup (236 ml) pitted Moroccan green olives

1 tablespoon (15 ml) chopped fresh parsley

Rice and Cheese Croquettes with Tomato and Green Olive Sauce

FOR THE CROQUETTES:

3 cups (708 ml) cooked and cooled short-grain rice

1 1/2 cups (354 ml) shredded mozzarella

1 1/2 teaspoons (7.5 ml) chopped fresh oregano leaves (or 1/2 teaspoon, 2.5 ml, dried)

3 large eggs

1/2 cup (118 ml) grated Parmesan

1 cup (236 ml) dry bread crumbs

Olive oil for frying

FOR THE SAUCE:

2 tablespoons (30 ml) olive oil

1/3 cup (79 ml) chopped onion

1 large clove garlic, peeled

28 ounce (828 ml) can whole plum tomatoes, with juice

2 tablespoons each (30 ml) chopped fresh basil and parsley (or 1 tablespoon, 15 ml, dried)

1 1/2 teaspoons (7.50 ml) chopped fresh oregano leaves (or 1/2 teaspoon, 2.5 ml, dried)

Salt and ground black pepper, 1/2 cup (118 ml) sliced, pitted green olives

*T*his dish can be used as a delicious starter, a side dish with meat or poultry, or the main course of a vegetarian meal. If you can't find short-grain rice, you may use medium grain, but long grain won't stick together well. Any kind of brine-cured green olive may be used.

Preparation time: 45 minutes, plus 1 to 3 hours chilling time

Making the croquettes: In a mixing bowl, combine the rice, mozzarella, and oregano. Mix well. Add 1 of the eggs and stir to thoroughly combine. In a small bowl, beat the remaining 2 eggs lightly. Place the Parmesan and bread crumbs on separate pieces of waxed paper. Line a tray or baking sheet with waxed paper.

Pick up some of the rice mixture in your hand and squeeze it until it holds together. (If it won't hold together, stir a tablespoon, *15 ml*, or so of flour into the rice mixture.) Form the lump in your hand into a patty and dredge it gently in the Parmesan, coating both sides. Shake off the excess. Coat the croquette with the beaten egg, then the bread crumbs, and place it on the prepared tray. Don't worry if the edges are ragged at this point. Continue making and coating croquettes until all the rice mixture is used. You should have 8 3-inch (*6 cm*) or 12 2-inch (*4 cm*) croquettes. Place the tray in the refrigerator and chill for 1 to 3 hours.

Making the sauce: Heat the oil in a saucepan over medium heat. Sauté the onion until tender and translucent, 3 to 5 minutes. Add the garlic and sauté 1 minute more. Add the tomatoes, basil, oregano, salt and pepper. Raise the heat and bring the sauce to a boil, breaking up the tomatoes with a spoon. Lower the heat and simmer, uncovered, occasionally mashing the tomatoes against the side of the pan to break them up, for 15 to 20 minutes, or until thickened somewhat. Stir in the olives and heat 2 minutes more. Serve immediately over fried croquettes or cover and set aside to be gently reheated at serving time.

Fry the croquettes. Heat 1/4 inch (*1 cm*) oil in a large skillet over medium-high heat. Remove the croquettes from the refrigerator and smooth any rough edges between your palms. Fry the croquettes until golden, 3 to 5 minutes a side. Drain on paper towels. Serve immediately with tomato-olive sauce, sprinkled with parsley.

Serves 4 as a main course, 6 as a starter or side dish

Wontons with Spicy Green Olive Sauce

FOR THE WONTONS:

3/4 pound (336 g) lean ground beef, lamb, veal, or pork

1/4 cup (59 ml) finely chopped scallion

1 clove garlic, minced

1/2 teaspoon (2.5 ml) ground cumin

Salt and freshly ground black pepper, to taste

12-ounce (336 g) package prepared square wonton wrappers, fresh or thawed frozen

FOR THE SAUCE:

1/2 cup (118 ml) olive oil

1/4 cup (59 ml) finely chopped onion

1 clove garlic, minced

2 teaspoons (10 ml) chili powder

1/4 teaspoon (1.25 ml) cayenne pepper, or to taste

1 cup (236 ml) sliced pitted green olives

Thinly sliced scallion greens for garnish, if desired

Wonton wrappers, as the dough is called, are too difficult to make at home without special equipment to get the dough thin enough. Fortunately, they're available in most supermarkets in the produce or frozen food sections. Don't be intimidated by them. They're very easy to use. And if you stick two together around a filling, you can make ravioli as well. Once you've tried them, you'll be experimenting with all kinds of fillings. This one is a dazzler!

Preparation time: 50 minutes

Making the wontons: In a small bowl combine all the wonton ingredients except the wrappers and mix well.

Lay a wonton wrapper on a smooth dry surface in front of you, with one corner toward you. (Make sure you only have one—they're very thin.) Place a level teaspoon (*5 ml*) of filling in the center of the wrapper. Dip your finger in water and run it along the two edges closest to you to dampen them. Bring the far corner over the filling to meet the point closest to you. Press the edges to seal. (The edges needn't meet exactly, as long as they're sealed all the way around.)

Dip your finger in the water again and dampen the top of one of the side points of the triangle you've made out of the wrapper. Bring the two points up and over the lump made by the filling and stick the damp side of the one down onto the top of the other, making what looks like a nurse's hat. Repeat with the other wrappers, making sure your fingers and surface are dry before starting the next. You may set up an assembly line and do several at once if desired.

At this point you may refrigerate the wontons several hours or freeze them.

Making the sauce: Heat the oil over medium heat. Sauté the onion until soft and translucent, about 2 minutes. Add the garlic, chili powder, and cayenne and sauté 30 seconds more. Add the olives and toss to coat. Heat through and keep over very low heat while you cook the wontons.

Shortly before serving time, bring a large pot of salted water to a boil. Drop in the wontons and simmer 3 to 4 minutes, or until filling is firm. Serve with sauce, garnished with scallion greens, if desired.

Makes about 5 dozen wontons, enough to serve 8 to 10

Linguini with Moroccan Oil-Cured Olive Sauce

1 cup (236 ml) loosely packed, pitted Moroccan oil-cured olives

2 tablespoons (30 ml) capers, rinsed and drained

1 1/2 tablespoons (22.5 ml) fresh rosemary leaves (or 1 1/2 teaspoons, 7.5 ml, dried)

1 clove garlic, whacked and peeled

2 anchovy fillets, rinsed and patted dry

1/2 teaspoon (2.5 ml) sugar

Freshly ground black pepper, to taste

2/3 cup plus 2 tablespoons (157 ml plus 30 ml) extra virgin olive oil

2 pounds fresh (900 g) or 1 1/2 pounds (675 g) dried linguini

6 ounces (168 g) firm sheep's milk cheese, shredded

2 scallions, thinly sliced

This gleaming black sauce resembling caviar makes a luscious topping for linguini. You may substitute other oil-cured olives or Italian roasted olives for the Moroccan, but choose a moist, not-too-dry variety. For the cheese, use a firm, not-too-salty sheep's milk cheese, such as Spanish Manchego, Italian Lacheso or Toscanello, or a French fromage des Pyrenees.

Preparation time: 30 minutes

Place the first seven ingredients, along with 2/3 cup (*157 ml*) oil in a blender or food processor. Process, pulsing on and off and scraping down the sides of the container, until well chopped and combined. Set aside. The mixture may have a tan liquid in it at this point.

Cook the linguini *al dente* in a large pot of boiling salted water. Drain and toss immediately with the remaining 2 tablespoons (*30 ml*) of oil.

Arrange linguini on a large serving platter or on individual plates. Scatter the cheese over the pasta. Stir the sauce well and spoon it on top, garnishing with the scallions. Serve immediately.

Serves 6

Potato Cakes with Manzanilla Olive Tartar Sauce

FOR THE TARTAR SAUCE:

3/4 cup (79 ml) mayonnaise,
preferably homemade

1 teaspoon (5 ml) Dijon mustard

1 tablespoon (15 ml) freshly
squeezed lemon juice

Freshly ground black pepper, to taste

1 teaspoon (5ml) finely chopped
fresh thyme leaves (or 1/2 teaspoon,
2.5 ml, dried)

1/3 cup (79 ml) finely chopped, pitted
Manzanilla olives

1 tablespoon (15 ml) finely chopped,
rinsed, and drained capers

4 scallions, green tops only, thinly
sliced (reserve white parts for cakes)

FOR THE POTATO CAKES:

2 pounds (900 g) medium-sized Idaho
or russet potatoes of uniform size

Thinly sliced, reserved white parts of
scallions (from tartar sauce)

1 large egg, lightly beaten

3 tablespoons (45 ml) heavy cream

Salt and freshly ground black pepper,
to taste

4 tablespoons (60 ml) olive oil

These luscious, golden brown cakes reach new heights when they're topped with a dollop of olive tartar sauce. Try the tartar sauce on fish or chicken, even poached turkey breast! Any other brine-cured green olive may be substituted.

Preparation time: 1 hour

Making the tartar sauce: In a small mixing bowl, whisk together the mayonnaise, mustard, lemon juice, and pepper. Add the thyme, olives, capers, and green scallion tops. Mix well, cover, and refrigerate until serving time. This may be made several hours to a day in advance.

Making the potato cakes: Drop the scrubbed, unpeeled potatoes into a large pot of boiling salted water. When the water returns to a boil, lower the heat to maintain a gentle boil, and cook uncovered, 20 minutes. Drain and plunge potatoes into cold water to stop cooking. They will not be completely cooked at this time.

When cooled, slip off skins and grate them on the large-holed side of a grater or with the large-holed grating disk in a food processor. Place the grated potatoes in a mixing bowl. Add the scallion whites and black pepper and mix well. Add the egg and cream and thoroughly combine. Wet your hands and shape the mixture into 12 cakes about 1/2-inch (*1 cm*) thick and 3 inches (*6 cm*) in diameter.

Warm a plate in an oven on low heat.

Heat 2 tablespoons (*30 ml*) of the oil in a large skillet over medium heat. Arrange half the cakes in the pan. Do not crowd. Brown cakes on both sides, about 3 to 5 minutes a side. Keep the cakes warm on the plate in the oven while you repeat with the remaining oil and cakes.

When they're all done, divide among serving plates and top with dollops of tartar sauce. Serve immediately.

Serves 4 as entrée, 6 as starter

CHAPTER 7

The Vegetarian Olive

Cheese Tortellini Salad with Escarole and California Sicilian-Style Olives

1 pound (454 g) fresh or frozen cheese tortellini

1/3 cup (79 ml) extra virgin olive oil

2 tablespoons (30 ml) freshly squeezed lemon juice

Salt and freshly ground black pepper, to taste

1/2 cup (118 ml) chopped red onion

1/4 cup (59 ml) pine nuts

1/4 cup (59 ml) golden raisins

1/2 cup (118 ml) California Sicilian-style olive pieces, cut from pits

1/4 pound (59 ml) escarole leaves, washed and dried

Legend has it that tortellini was invented by a Bolognese innkeeper who had sneaked a peek at Venus's navel and was so impressed, he tried to recreate it in a pasta. This wonderful salad is equally appropriate as a lunch or summer dinner entrée, or as a course in a larger dinner. Other green, brine-cured olives may be used if desired.

Preparation time: 25 minutes

Cook the tortellini *al dente* in a large pot of boiling salted water. Drain, rinse under cold running water until cool. Drain again.

Combine the oil, lemon juice, salt and pepper in a salad bowl. Whisk until well mixed. Add the tortellini to the bowl, along with the onion, pine nuts, raisins, and olives and toss well to coat.

Arrange escarole leaves on serving plates. Divide the tortellini mixture among them and serve immediately.

Serves 4 to 6

Tomato Soup with Red Wine and Kalamata Olives

3 pounds (1.1 kg) fresh tomatoes, sliced (or 40 ounces, 1.1 kg, canned tomatoes)

1/2 cup (118 ml) chopped onion

3 cloves garlic, minced

3 cups (708 ml) high quality Bordeaux

1 tablespoon (15 ml) dark brown sugar

1 tablespoon (15 ml) Worcestershire sauce

1 tablespoon (15 ml) chopped fresh dill (or 1 teaspoon, 5 ml, dried)

2 tablespoons (30 ml) tomato paste

3 sprigs fresh parsley

1 small bay leaf

Salt and freshly ground black pepper, to taste

1 cup (236 ml) pitted and sliced Kalamata olives

1 1/2 tablespoons (22.5 ml) chopped fresh dill, for garnish

This rich, delicious soup is equally good hot or chilled. It can be made in advance, but don't add the olives and fresh dill until you're ready to serve it. You may substitute other mild brine-cured black olives if desired; Alphonsos work quite well. Serve with a crusty French bread for your guests to dunk in the luscious broth. If you can't get fresh tomatoes, used canned. A high quality wine is essential for this recipe.

Preparation time: 45 minutes, plus chilling time, if desired

Place all ingredients, except the olives and the dill for garnish, in a 3 1/2- to 4-quart (3.7 l) nonreactive pot. Bring to a boil, lower heat, cover, and simmer 20 to 30 minutes, until the tomatoes are tender.

Pour the soup through a sieve, pressing the solids with the back of a spoon to extract as much juice as possible. Return the strained liquid to the cleaned soup pot and heat through. Or, if you desire to serve it cold, cover, cool, and refrigerate several hours or overnight.

When ready to serve, reheat over medium heat or serve cold. Divide soup among serving bowls, distribute olives among the bowls, and top each with a sprinkling of dill.

Serves 4 to 6

Chick Peas with Spinach and Royal Victoria Olives

2 cups (472 ml) cooked chick peas (1 cup, 236 ml, dried peas that have been cooked and drained or 1 19-ounce, 532 g, can, rinsed and drained)

1/2 cup (118 ml) thinly sliced 1 1/2-inch (3 cm) long strips of red bell pepper

1 tablespoon (15 ml) finely chopped fresh mint leaves

1/2 cup (118 ml) pitted Royal Victoria olive pieces

1/2 pound (227 g) fresh spinach leaves, chopped

1/4 cup (59 ml) extra virgin olive oil

2 tablespoons (30 ml) freshly squeezed lemon juice

1 1/2 teaspoons (7.5 ml) yellow mustard seeds

Dash of hot sauce, or to taste

Salt and freshly ground black pepper, to taste

*T*his is a simple, farmhouse-style salad that can stand alone as a luncheon entrée or share the bill at dinner. Other brine-cured black olives such as Alphonso, Kalamata, or Greek black may be substituted.

Preparation time: 10 minutes

Place the chick peas, bell pepper, mint, olives, and spinach in a salad bowl.

In a small bowl, whisk together the remaining ingredients and pour them over the salad. Toss to coat and serve.

Serves 4

Tubetti with Lemon, Black Beans, and Manzanilla Olives

Here's another dish that can stand alone as a luncheon entrée or serve as one course or side dish of a larger dinner. Dry Jack cheese is not the Monterey Jack cheese you see in the market, but an aged, gratable version invented during the 1940s. It's hard to find, but worth a try. You may substitute Parmigiano Reggiano or Pecorino Romano. You may use any other brine-cured green olive as an alternative.

Preparation time: 30 minutes

Place the beans, olives, onion, oregano, and oil in a large mixing bowl.

Remove the zest from the lemon with a vegetable peeler, chop coarsely, and add it to the bowl. Squeeze the lemon and add the juice to the bowl. Add salt and pepper to taste and toss to combine.

Cook tubetti *al dente* in a large pot of salted boiling water. Drain and add immediately to the bowl of other ingredients. Toss gently to thoroughly combine. Serve at room temperature with grated cheese.

Serves 6

1 1/2 cups (354 ml) cooked black beans (3/4 cup, 177 ml, dried, cooked and drained, or one 15-ounce (420 g) can, rinsed and drained)

1 cup (236 ml) sliced Manzanilla olives stuffed with pimiento

1 small red onion, chopped

1 tablespoon (15 ml) chopped fresh oregano leaves
(or 1 teaspoon (15 ml) dried)

1/4 cup (59 ml) extra virgin olive oil

1 large lemon

Salt and freshly ground black pepper, to taste

8 ounces (224 g) tubetti

Grated dry Jack cheese

Greek Salad with Feta Cheese and Kalamata Olives

8 cups (2 l) torn mixed greens

1 small cucumber, thinly sliced

1 medium-sized tomato, cut into thin wedges

1 small green bell pepper, thinly sliced and seeded

8 red radishes, thinly sliced

8 to 12 pepperoncini (optional)

24 unpitted Kalamatas

8 to 12 dolmati (stuffed grape leaves, optional)

6 ounces (168 g) Feta cheese

4 teaspoons (20 ml) finely chopped fresh oregano leaves (or 1 1/2 teaspoons, 7.5 ml, dried)

1/2 cup (118 ml) extra virgin olive oil

4 to 6 tablespoons (60 to 90 ml) red wine vinegar

Salt and freshly ground black pepper, to taste

This salad can be made large enough to be a whole meal or small enough to be a course in a large repast. You'll need to serve something else with it, but not four or five courses. Feel free to adjust the size. Some of the ingredients may be unfamiliar to you. Pepperoncini are small, pale green mild peppers, available in most markets bottled in brine. Dolmati are grape leaves, stuffed with rice, spices, and sometimes, lamb. They are best fresh, but are also available in cans and jars. Kalamata olives are traditional, but you may substitute Greek black, Gaeta, Naphlion, Niçoise, or Royal Victoria.

Preparation time: 5 minutes

Divide the greens among four plates, or spread in a wide, shallow serving bowl. Scatter the cucumber, tomato, radish, and bell pepper slices over them. Divide up the pepperoncini, Kalamatas, and dolmati among the plates, or spread out around the serving bowl. Crumble Feta in the center, sprinkle with oregano, and drizzle with oil, then vinegar.

Season with salt and pepper to taste and serve. Pass the oil and vinegar to anyone who wants more. (You may choose to allow each person to add their own oil and vinegar at the table, rather than putting it on yourself.)

Serves 4

Fresh Herb Risotto with Naphlion Olives

3 tablespoons (45 ml) extra virgin olive oil

1/2 cup (118 ml) chopped, pitted Naphlion olives

3 tablespoons (45 ml) chopped fresh herbs (parsley, basil, mint, chives, rosemary, marjoram, oregano, or thyme may be used in any combination)

6 cups (1.4 l) chicken broth

2 tablespoons (30 ml) olive oil

1 small onion, finely chopped

2 cloves garlic, minced

1 cup (236 ml) dry white wine

2 cups (472 ml) Arborio rice

Freshly ground black pepper, to taste

1/3 cup (79 ml) grated Parmesan cheese

This is a delicious way to use up the ends of all those packages of fresh herbs you may have in your refrigerator, if you aren't lucky enough to have a place to grow them. If you do grow your own herbs, this recipe is great for keeping those plants pinched back. Fresh herbs are essential here, but you may substitute Niçoise for Naphlion Olives. Carnaroli or Vialone Nano rices may also be used, but generally, Arborio is the easiest to find. No other substitutions, please.

Preparation time: 50 minutes

In a small bowl, combine the extra virgin oil, the olives, and the herbs. Stir to combine and set aside.

In a saucepan, heat the broth to steaming.

In a second, large, heavy-bottomed saucepan, sauté the onion in the olive oil over medium heat until tender and translucent, about 3 minutes. Add the garlic and sauté 1 more minute. Add the wine, raise the heat, and boil until reduced by about half.

Lower the heat to low, add the rice, and stir well. Add about 1/2 cup (*118 ml*) of broth and stir until absorbed. Continue to add broth at the same rate until you've used it all, and the rice is cooked *al dente*, but is still liquid enough to be creamy, about 30 minutes.

Remove from the heat and season with pepper. Stir in the Parmesan cheese and the reserved herb-olive mixture. Cover and let sit a couple of minutes before serving.

Serves 6

Spicy Penne with Cauliflower and Alphonso Olives

his dish works equally well as a vegetarian entrée or a side dish. The Alphonsos add a lovely touch of color, staining the pasta and cauliflower purple. However, if you can't find them, you may substitute Greek Black, Kalamata, Gaeta, or Royal Victoria.

Preparation time: 35 minutes

Bring a large pot of water to a rapid boil. Heat the olive oil in a small pan over medium heat. When hot, add the garlic and red pepper flakes. Stir. Remove from the heat and set aside.

Separate the cauliflower into florets, then cut or break the florets into 1-inch (2.5 cm) pieces. Set aside.

When the pot of water reaches a boil, add 1 tablespoon (15 ml) of salt and the penne. Return to the boil, stirring frequently, and once it has resumed boiling, cook 6 minutes. Add the cauliflower and continue to cook for 4 to 6 minutes more, until the penne is cooked *al dente*. Drain pasta and cauliflower and transfer to a large bowl.

Toss immediately with the extra virgin olive oil, the reserved garlic-pepper oil, the lemon juice, rosemary, parsley, olives, Parmesan, and black pepper until well combined. Serve immediately with additional Parmesan to pass.

Serves 6 to 8

2 tablespoons (30 ml) olive oil

2 cloves garlic, minced

3/4 teaspoon (3.75 ml) crushed red pepper flakes

1 medium-sized head of cauliflower

1 tablespoon (15 ml) salt

1 pound (454 g) dried penne

1/2 cup (118 ml) extra virgin olive oil

2 tablespoons (30 ml) freshly squeezed lemon juice

1 1/2 tablespoons (22.5 ml) chopped fresh rosemary (or 2 teaspoons, 10 ml, dried)

1/4 cup (59 ml) chopped fresh parsley

1 cup (236 ml) sliced, pitted Alphonso olives

1/2 cup (118 ml) freshly grated Parmesan cheese, plus more for the table

Freshly ground black pepper, to taste

Lentils with Alphonso Olive Rouille

FOR THE LENTILS:

3 tablespoons (45 ml) olive oil

1/4 cup (59 ml) finely chopped shallots

1/2 cup (118 ml) finely chopped celery

1/2 cup (118 ml) finely chopped carrots

2 cups (472 ml) dried lentils, picked over, rinsed, and drained

4 cups (3.8 l) chicken broth

A bouquet garni of 1 bay leaf and 3 sprigs each of fresh oregano and parsley, tied together

Salt and freshly ground black pepper, to taste

FOR THE ROUILLE:

2 tablespoons (30 ml) red wine vinegar

2/3 cup (157 ml) soft fresh bread crumbs

2 cloves garlic, whacked and peeled

1/2 cup (118 ml) pitted Alphonso olives

2 hot red peppers, seeded and chopped, or 2 teaspoons (10 ml) Tabasco® sauce

5 tablespoons (75 ml) extra virgin olive oil

*L*entils just might be the oldest of the legumes. *Their earthy taste and the incredible ease with which they are prepared makes them a favorite the world over. You may use the common and easy-to-find green or brown lentils; the harder to find, larger variety of the red lentil; or the more expensive peppery-flavored French lentil. A rouille (pronounced roo-EE) is a spicy French paste used traditionally to perk up fish dishes. It's traditionally pounded to a paste and contains no olives. The Alphonsos make the rouille a very nice purple color, but you may use other ripe or green olives if you desire. The rouille can also be used as a condiment on dozens of things, from sandwiches to vegetables.*

Preparation time: 45 minutes

Heat the oil in a pan over medium-high heat. Sauté the shallots, celery, and carrots until the shallots are soft and translucent, 2 to 3 minutes. Add the lentils, broth, and bouquet garni and bring to a boil. Cover, lower the heat and simmer 15 to 25 minutes, depending on the variety, until the lentils are tender but still hold their shape. Discard the bouquet garni and season to taste with salt and pepper. Serve hot.

While the lentils cook, make the rouille.

Combine the vinegar and bread crumbs. Place them with all other rouille ingredients except the olive oil in a blender or food processor. Process to chop everything fine, scraping down sides of blender or processor. With the machine running, pour in the oil in a thin, steady stream, until it is all incorporated and smooth.

Serve lentils with a small dollop of rouille on each serving, and pass a small bowl around for guests to add extra.

Serves 6

Beet Salad with Oranges and Oil-Cured Olives

T his is a beautiful salad, combining the beet and orange salads of America and Europe with the orange and black olive salads of Morocco. Use smaller beets, about 2 inches in diameter, since larger ones tend to get tougher. Any dry-roasted, oil-, or dry-cured olive will do. Just pull them apart to pit them. You may serve this on a bed of lettuce leaves or without, as you wish.

Preparation time: 45 minutes

Bring a pot of water to a boil, add beets and boil gently, 25 to 30 minutes or until tender enough to be easily pierced with a knife. Plunge into cold water and allow to cool completely. Peel or scrape skins from beets with fingers or edge of knife. Halve and slice.

Place the beets in a salad bowl with the oranges, cucumber, red onion, olives, parsley, and dill.

In a small bowl or jar, whisk or shake together the lemon juice, any orange juice released while peeling, the olive oil, fennel seeds, and salt and pepper. Pour over the salad and toss to coat.

Serve immediately as is or on a bed of lettuce leaves.

Serves 4

4 2-inch (5 cm) beets, roots untrimmed, stems trimmed 2 inches (5 cm) above beets

2 oranges, peeled, sectioned, and seeded, any juice reserved

1 small cucumber, peeled, halved lengthwise, seeded and sliced

1 small red onion, halved and thinly sliced

2/3 cup (157 ml) pitted oil-cured olives

2 tablespoons (30 ml) chopped fresh parsley

2 tablespoons (30 ml) chopped fresh dill

1 tablespoon (15 ml) freshly squeezed lemon juice

1/3 cup (79 ml) extra virgin olive oil

1 teaspoon (5 ml) fennel seeds, crushed in a mortar

Salt and freshly ground black pepper, to taste

CHAPTER 8

The Oceanic Olive

Mussels with Fennel and San Remo Olives

If you love mussels, but you've gotten squeamish about them because of ocean-water impurities and grit in the bite, join the modern world. There are now mussel farms that raise sand-free mussels in clean waters. Look for them in your local seafood store. Other mild, brine-cured ripe olives, such as Kalamata or Niçoise, may be substituted.

Preparation time: 25 minutes, plus 2 hours soaking time

Discard any mussels that don't close tightly after being handled and any that are too light (dead), or too heavy (full of sand). Then scrub the mussel shells with a stiff brush and pull or scrape off any beards protruding from the shells. Place the mussels in a large bowl of fresh, cool water for about 2 hours, changing the water twice to remove any sand. Drain in a colander and rinse thoroughly again.

Next, trim the tops from the fennel, reserving any feathery green parts for garnish. Quarter the bulbs and cut out the central core. Slice the pieces crosswise and set aside.

When ready to eat, put the wine, lemon juice, reserved fennel, shallots, thyme, parsley, salt and pepper in a large skillet or pan. Bring to a boil and boil 2 minutes. Add the mussels and olives, cover tightly and boil for about 5 minutes, holding the lid on and shaking the pan occasionally to make them cook evenly.

With a slotted spoon remove mussels, fennel, and olives. Spoon or pour liquid into bowls. Drizzle with olive oil and sprinkle with chopped reserved fennel tops.

Serves 4

3 pounds (1.35 kg) fresh mussels

2 small fennel bulbs

2 cups (472 ml) dry white wine

1 tablespoon (15 ml) lemon juice

1/4 cup (59 ml) chopped shallots

1 1/2 teaspoons (7.5 ml) chopped fresh thyme leaves (or 1/2 teaspoon, 2.5 ml, dried)

1 tablespoon (15 ml) chopped fresh parsley leaves

Salt and freshly ground black pepper, to taste

1 cup (236 ml) unpitted San Remo olives

3 to 4 tablespoons (45 to 60 ml) extra virgin olive oil

Marinated Squid Salad with Chilies and Picholine Olives

11/2 pounds (675 g) cleaned squid

11/2 cups (354 ml) dry white wine

1 teaspoon (5 ml) celery seeds

2 tablespoons (30 ml) grated onion

1/2 cup (118 ml) extra virgin olive oil

1/4 cup (59 ml) freshly squeezed lemon juice

1 teaspoon (5 ml) grated lemon zest

1 clove garlic, minced

3 hot chilies, such as jalapeño or serrano, seeded and chopped

4 tablespoons (60 ml) chopped fresh dill

Salt and freshly ground black pepper, to taste

8 cups (1.9 l) torn mixed lettuce leaves (such as bibb, Boston, leaf, oak leaf, radicchio, endive, etc.)

*S*quid is one of the most overlooked best food buys. Many people are afraid of it because of the name (so call it "calamari"), or because they think it tastes like rubber bands (only when cooked improperly). Cooked correctly, squid is pure joy—high in protein, low in fat, mild, and delicious. It's also about the least expensive seafood available, even when already cleaned. This wonderful salad is slightly spicy, light, and cool—perfect summer fare. Other green olives may be substituted for the Picholines, which can be pitted or not, as you wish. Remember to warn your guests if you don't pit them!

Preparation time: 20 minutes, plus 2 hours marinating time

1 small onion, thinly sliced

1 small cucumber, peeled and thinly sliced

Half pint (approx. 15 to 20) small red or yellow cherry tomatoes, halved

2/3 cup (157 ml) Picholine olives, pitted or not, as you like

2 tablespoons (30 ml) chopped fresh parsley leaves

2 tablespoons (30 ml) chopped fresh mint leaves

Rinse squid well. Cut into 1/4-inch (.6 cm) rings, cut off long tentacles, and quarter each set of tentacles.

Place the wine, celery seed, and grated onion in a pot and bring to a boil over high heat. Boil one minute and add squid. Return to boil, still over high heat, and cook, stirring constantly 30 seconds, or until all the squid pieces are opaque and white. Remove the squid from the liquid with a slotted spoon. Set liquid aside.

Toss squid immediately with oil, lemon juice, lemon zest, garlic, chilies, 2 tablespoons (30 ml) of the dill, and salt and pepper. Cover and refrigerate about 2 hours.

Return the pan of cooking liquid to the stove over high heat. Boil until reduced to about 2 tablespoons (30 ml) of liquid, onions, and seeds. Pour into small bowl and cool to room temperature. When cool, toss with squid, then recover squid and return it to the refrigerator for the remainder of the 2 hours.

At serving time, divide lettuce leaves among serving plates. Place the remaining ingredients in a bowl. Add the squid with the marinade and toss. Divide the squid mixture among the plates, scattering over the lettuce leaves, drizzle with any leftover marinade, and serve.

Serves 4 to 6

Grilled Mahi-Mahi with Tangy Black Olive Sauce

1 cup (236 ml) finely chopped, pitted black olives

2 tablespoons (30 ml) finely chopped shallots

1/2 medium-sized red bell pepper, seeded and finely chopped

2 finely chopped jalapeño or serrano peppers, seeded (unless you want the dish to be very hot)

Grated zest and juice of a large lemon

1 large clove garlic, minced

1/2 teaspoon (2.5 ml) ground coriander

1/2 teaspoon (2.5 ml) ground cumin

3 tablespoons (45 ml) extra virgin olive oil

4 mahi-mahi steaks, 1-inch thick, about 5 to 7 ounces (140 to 195 g) each

3 tablespoons (45 ml) olive oil

Salt and freshly ground black pepper, to taste

Mild, white-fleshed fish such as mahi-mahi go perfectly with flavorful sauces like this one. You may use any black olive, from Greek black to Niçoise, here, but stay away from the bitterest varieties.

Preparation time: 30 minutes, plus one hour sitting time

In a small bowl combine the first 9 ingredients. Mix well and allow to sit, covered, at room temperature for 1 hour.

Rinse fish steaks, pat dry, and brush with olive oil. Season to taste with salt and black pepper. Grill over hot coals or under broiler about 10 minutes, turning once halfway through. Serve garnished with black olive sauce.

Serves 4

Herbed Swordfish with Naphlion Olives

Swordfish is a great favorite among seafood lovers. Its wonderfully thick steaks, mild, firm flesh, and low fat content adapt easily to a number of cooking methods. This is one of my favorite ways to fix swordfish steaks, coated with fresh herbs and garnished with intense Naphlion olives. There really aren't other olives like Naphlion, but you may substitute Arbequina, Italian San Remo, or cracked Provençal. Swordfish is generally available all over the world, but you can also use tilefish, halibut, shark, or any other mild, white-fleshed fish available in steaks. Fresh herbs really brighten this dish, so try to use them if at all possible. You may choose to grill as well.

Preparation time: 25 minutes

Preheat the broiler.

In a small bowl, whisk together the yolk, oil, and juices. Stir in the orange zest, herbs, salt and pepper.

Place the steaks in the center of an oiled broiler rack. Place about a tablespoon (*15 ml*) of the herb mixture on top of each and smear it all over the surface. Broil 3 to 5 inches (*8 to 12 cm*) from the flame for 3 to 5 minutes, or until lightly browned.

Carefully, turn steaks over and divide the remaining herb mixture among them, about a tablespoon (*15 ml*) each. Broil again from 3 to 5 minutes, until lightly browned. Remove to serving platter or plates and top with chopped olives. Serve immediately.

Serves 4

1 large egg yolk

1/2 cup (118 ml) olive oil

1 tablespoon (15 ml) freshly squeezed orange juice

1 teaspoon (5 ml) freshly squeezed lemon juice

1 teaspoon (5 ml) grated orange zest

2 teaspoons (10 ml) finely chopped fresh or frozen chives

2 teaspoons (10 ml) finely chopped fresh thyme leaves (or 3/4 teaspoon, 3.75 ml, dried)

2 teaspoons (10 ml) finely chopped fresh parsley

Salt and freshly ground black pepper, to taste

4 swordfish steaks, 1-inch to 1 1/4-inches (2.5 to 3 cm) thick, 6 to 8 ounces (170 to 225 g) apiece

1/2 cup (118 ml) chopped, pitted Naphlion olives

Seviche with Baena Oil

1 pound (454 g) very fresh, firm, white-fleshed saltwater fish, such as red snapper, pompano, sole, cod, or halibut

2/3 cup (157 ml) freshly squeezed lime juice

2 jalapeño or serrano peppers, seeded and minced

1 clove garlic, minced

1 1/2 teaspoons (7.5 ml) bottled white horseradish

1 small red onion, chopped

1 medium-sized tomato, seeded and chopped

3 tablespoons (45 ml) finely chopped cilantro leaves

1/3 cup (79 ml) extra virgin Baena oil

Salt and freshly ground black pepper, to taste

Lime wedges for garnish

Seviche (also spelled ceviche and cebiche) is a traditional appetizer of Central and South America that uses the acidity of citrus juice to "cook" fish or shellfish. Baena is a southern province of Cordoba, an area of south-central Spain. It is renowned for producing the finest oils of the region. It is one of the four labels of origin recognized by the Spanish olive oil industry. If you cannot find it, you may substitute another good quality, fruity extra virgin oil.

Preparation time: 30 minutes, plus 6 hours to overnight marinating time

Trim the fish of all skin, bones, and fat. Cut into 1-inch (2.5 cm) cubes. Place in a glass bowl, add the lime juice, toss to coat, cover, and refrigerate from 6 hours to overnight.

About 30 minutes before serving, drain the fish and place it in a serving bowl. Add the remaining ingredients, except the lime wedges, and gently fold together until well combined. Cover and refrigerate 20 to 30 minutes to combine flavors. Serve garnished with lime wedges.

Serves 4

CHAPTER 9

The Beefy Olive

Veal Piccata with Niçoise Olives

This is a traditional Italian veal dish that is usually made with capers. My version entails some EEC cooperation, since it incorporates French olives. This dish is equally good prepared with flattened chicken breasts, and with any olive you prefer. Don't try making it for a large crowd, however (four servings works best). Pitting Niçoises, which can be time consuming, isn't mandatory, but it makes the dish easier to eat.

Preparation time: 35 minutes

Heat a serving plate in a low-temperature oven.

Place the cutlets several inches apart between two sheets of waxed paper or plastic wrap and pound to between an 1/8-inch and 1/4-inch (.32 cm and .63 cm) thickness (or get your butcher to do it for you).

Season the cutlets with salt and pepper, and dredge in flour to coat.

Heat half of the oil and butter in a large, nonreactive skillet over medium-high heat. Place the cutlets in without crowding them, and brown lightly on each side (about 2 to 3 minutes per side). Remove the cutlets to the warm serving plate as they are done, keeping them warm in the low-temperature oven. Add more cutlets to the pan with more oil and butter as needed.

When the cutlets are all done, add the wine, raise the heat, and scrape up the browned bits from the pan. Boil until reduced by about half, 4 to 5 minutes. Add the lemon juice and olives and heat through. Pour over the veal, sprinkle with parsley, and serve.

Serves 4

1 1/2 pounds (680 g) veal cutlets

Salt and freshly ground black pepper, to taste

Flour for dredging

3 tablespoons (45 ml) olive oil

1 tablespoon (15 ml) unsalted butter

1 cup (236 ml) dry white wine

3 tablespoons (45 ml) freshly squeezed lemon juice

1/3 cup (79 ml) pitted Niçoise olives (may be left unpitted, but warn your guests)

1 tablespoon (15 ml) finely chopped fresh parsley leaves

Beef and Manzanilla Olive Empanadas

FOR THE DOUGH:

4 cups (1 l) flour

1 teaspoon (5 ml) salt

6 tablespoons (90 ml) vegetable shortening

2 large eggs

1/2 cup (118 ml) cold water

Olive oil for brushing tops or deep frying, if desired

FOR THE FILLING:

1 tablespoon (15 ml) olive oil

1 small onion, chopped

3/4 pound (335 g) lean ground beef

2 scallions, thinly sliced

2 hard-boiled eggs, peeled and chopped

1/2 cup (118 ml) golden raisins, plumped in hot water to cover for 30 minutes

1/2 cup (118 ml) chopped, pitted Manzanilla olives

3 tablespoons (45 ml) extra virgin olive oil

2 teaspoons (10 ml) ground cumin

1/4 teaspoon (1.25 ml) cayenne

Empanadas are Spanish turnovers. I was introduced to this wonderful version by a friend from Argentina. You may make larger empanadas, great for luncheon or picnics, or smaller ones, ideal for hors d'oeuvre trays or as starters. You may also deep fry the empanadas (the more traditional way) or bake them (the healthier way). Any green olive may be substituted.

Preparation time: 1 hour 20 minutes

By hand: Place the flour and salt in mixing bowl. Cut in the shortening until thoroughly dispersed. Mix in the egg, then the cold water. If it's not moist enough to hold together, add more water, 1 tablespoon (*15 ml*) at a time. When the dough holds together, form it into 2 balls and dust with flour. Wrap each in wax paper and refrigerate at least 30 minutes, or until the filling is ready.

With a food processor: Make dough in two batches, with half the ingredients in each. Place half the flour and salt in the processor. Process until well dispersed. Add the egg, close the lid, and with the machine running, add 1/4 cup (*59 ml*) water through the chute. If the dough doesn't form a ball, add more, 1 teaspoon (*5 ml*) at a time. When a ball forms, dust it with flour, wrap it in wax paper, and refrigerate for at least 30 minutes, or until filling is ready. Repeat with the second half of the ingredients.

Heat the olive oil in a skillet over medium-high heat. Sauté the onion until soft and translucent, 2 to 3 minutes. Add the beef and brown it, chopping it up with a spoon. When no pink remains, pour off any fat and transfer the

skillet contents to a bowl. Add the remaining ingredients and mix well. Allow the filling to cool before using.

For the assembly: Preheat the oven to 450°F (232°C). Lightly oil two baking sheets.

Take one ball of dough out of refrigerator and place it on a lightly floured surface. Roll it out to 1/8-inch (31 mm) thickness and cut out 4-inch (6.45 cm) circles with an empty coffee can for small empanadas (a biscuit cutter for really small ones), or 7-inch (17.78 cm) circles, cutting around a pan lid with a sharp knife for large empanadas.

Dip a finger or brush in water and run it around the outer 1/2 inch (1.27 cm) of the dough circle. Place a heaping tablespoon (15 ml) filling for small circles or 1/4 cup (59 ml) for larger circles in the center of the dough circle. Fold the dough over and press it around the edges to seal. Using the tines of a fork, seal the edges, then pierce the top to vent any steam.

Re-form any excess dough by squeezing or kneading and re-roll. Repeat with the second ball of dough until it's all used up.

Place the empanadas on the prepared baking sheets, brush with olive oil, and bake in the preheated oven 15 to 20 minutes, or until golden brown. Alternately deep fry until golden brown and drain on paper towels.

Makes 12 large or 24 small empanadas

Beef, Tomato, and Niçoise Olive Ragout

H ere's a very thick concoction of complex flavors that develop with long, slow cooking. The Niçoises don't have to be pitted—but even though it's less authentic, pitted olives make the dish easier to eat. Gaeta, Naphlion, San Remo, Kalamata, or even cracked Provençals could be substituted. A good wine and a double-rich broth are very helpful here. If you don't have homemade broth, use a can of low-sodium broth and reduce it by half. Serve with crusty French bread or boiled potatoes.

Preparation time: 3 hours 15 minutes

4 pounds (1.8 kg) lean boneless beef stew meat, cut into 2-inch (5 cm) cubes

2 to 3 tablespoons (30 to 45 ml) olive oil

3/8 lb (168 g) lean smoked sliced bacon, cut into 1-inch (2.5 cm) lengths

2 large onions, coarsely chopped

3 medium-sized carrots, scraped and cut into 1-inch (2.5 cm) lengths

4 medium-sized cloves garlic, whacked and peeled

2 strips orange zest, each about 1 inch by 3 inches (2.5 cm by 7.6 cm), removed with a vegetable peeler

1 cup (236 ml) rich beef broth

4 large tomatoes, peeled, seeded, and coarsely chopped

A bouquet garni consisting of 1 bay leaf and 3 sprigs each fresh thyme and parsley

1 cup (236 ml) young dry red wine, such as zinfandel, syrah, or Beaujolais

1/4 cup (59 ml) cognac or brandy

Salt and freshly ground black pepper, to taste

1 cup (236 ml) loosely packed, pitted Niçoise olives

3 tablespoons (45 ml) finely chopped fresh parsley leaves

Dry the meat cubes thoroughly.

Heat a large skillet over medium-high heat. Add 2 tablespoons (30 ml) of oil and swirl to coat the bottom. Add enough beef cubes to fit comfortably in one layer. Brown the meat on all sides, removing the pieces to a flameproof casserole as they're done. Add more meat as there is room and more oil as needed until all the meat is done.

Preheat the oven to 325°F (163°C).

Pour off any accumulated fat from the skillet. Add the bacon and sauté until it begins to brown. Add the onions, carrots, garlic, and orange zest, and raise the heat slightly. Continue to sauté, stirring frequently, until the edges of the onion are golden brown, 7 to 8 minutes.

Add the contents of the skillet to the casserole. Pour the broth into the skillet and heat it, scraping up any browned bits with a wooden spoon. Pour the steaming broth into the casserole, along with the tomatoes, bouquet garni, wine, cognac, salt and pepper. Stir to combine.

Bring the casserole to a simmer over medium-high heat. Cover tightly and bake in the preheated oven about 2 hours, or until the meat is tender.

Remove from oven, add olives, stirring gently to distribute them. Check seasoning, re-cover, and return to the oven for 20 more minutes. Remove bouquet garni and serve, garnished with parsley.

Serves 6

Westphalian Ham and Picholine Olive Quiche

1 9-inch (23 cm) pie or tart shell

1 tablespoon (15 ml) olive oil

1 small onion, thinly sliced

1/4 lb (112 g) thinly sliced Westphalian ham

1/2 cup (118 ml) pitted Picholine olive pieces

1/2 teaspoon (2.5 ml) freshly ground black pepper

4 large eggs

1 cup (236 ml) light cream, half-and-half, or evaporated milk

Pinch of freshly grated nutmeg

Westphalian ham is a very fine product made from pigs raised on acorns in Germany's Westphalia forest. It is cured, then slowly smoked with beech wood and juniper. It has a delicious smoky, rich taste that marries beautifully with the Picholine olives. It is somewhat salty, though, so you won't need any additional salt. Picholines are best pitted by mashing under the heel of your hand or the side of a knife, as you would a garlic clove. You may substitute any other green, brine-cured olive.

Preparation time: 50 minutes

Preheat the oven to 425°F (218°C).

Place a piece of aluminum foil over the raw crust dough in the pie pan. Fill with pie weights, raw rice, or dried beans and bake on the lowest shelf of the oven for 10 to 12 minutes. Remove the foil and weights and cook 3 to 4 minutes more to dry the crust out. Cool completely on a wire rack.

Reduce the oven temperature to 375°F (190°C).

Heat the oil in a small skillet over medium heat and sauté the onion until it is tender and translucent, about 3 minutes. Set aside.

Arrange the ham slices over the bottom and up the sides of the cooled crust. Scatter the onion over the ham, then the olives and the pepper.

In a mixing bowl, whisk the eggs until pale yellow. Add the cream and nutmeg and whisk until thoroughly combined. Pour over the other ingredients in the shell, filling to within 1/8 inch (30 mm) of the top. (You may want to add the last of it after you have set it in the oven.)

Place on the oven's center rack and bake 25 to 30 minutes, or until a knife inserted in the center comes out clean.

Serve warm or at room temperature.

Serves 6

Chorizos, Red Beans, and Rice, Drizzled with Oil

1 pound (450 g) dried
small red beans

3 cups (708 ml) chicken or
vegetable broth

8 ounces (224 g) chorizos

1 large onion, chopped

3 cloves garlic, finely chopped

1 large fresh ripe tomato, peeled,
seeded and chopped

Salt and freshly ground black
pepper, to taste

3 tablespoons (45 ml) chopped
fresh cilantro or parsley leaves

3 cups (708 ml) hot cooked rice

Chopped or sliced green bell
pepper for garnish

Extra virgin olive oil for drizzling

Hot sauce for the table

*C*horizos are spicy Spanish and Mexican sausages made from pork and flavored with garlic and chili powder, among other things. They have a taste all their own, so any substitution will change the flavor. If you can't find them, you may use Cajun andouille or Polish kielbasa, or any spicy garlic sausage. Small red beans are also sold as "colorado chicos." Like any bean dish, this is even better leftover the next day.

Preparation time: 1 hour 30 minutes, plus soaking time

Pick over the beans and rinse thoroughly. Place in a large pot, with 2 inches (5 cm) water, cover, and let sit overnight. Alternatively, but less desirably, bring to a boil for 2 minutes, remove from heat, cover, and let sit 2 hours, then proceed.

The next day, or after boiling and soaking, drain the beans, return them to the pot with the broth, bring to a boil, cover, reduce heat, and simmer for about 1 hour, until they're tender but still hold their shape.

Before the hour is up, heat a skillet over medium heat, peel the casings from the chorizos if they are tough, slice the sausages, and add them to the skillet. Sauté several minutes until they are lightly browned and have given off much of their fat. Pour off the fat (or blot it up with paper towels) and add the onions, sautéing until they are soft and translucent, 3 to 5 minutes. Add the garlic and tomato, cook 2 minutes more, and remove from heat.

When the beans are tender, but still firm, add the skillet contents to the pot of beans, mixing well. Season to taste with salt and pepper. Raise the heat slightly (if necessary to

maintain a simmer) and simmer, uncovered for about 20 minutes, or until thickened somewhat. There should still be some liquid, however, especially if you are cooking them ahead of time. They will absorb more liquid while cooling. If cooking ahead or for a left-over meal, reheat gently when ready to serve.

At serving time, stir cilantro or parsley into the hot beans and serve with rice, garnished with green pepper, and drizzled lightly with oil. Use Hot Pepper Oil (page 73) or pass the hot sauce, separately.

Serves 6 to 8

CHAPTER 10

The Baked Olive

Giant Almond Cookies

These extra-large cookies are as much a pleasure to look at as they are to eat. Almond cookies have long been a tradition in cultures as varied as Scandinavian and Chinese. Almonds, ground and otherwise, are the world's most grown and eaten nut, and are used to satisfy sweet appetites the world over. It was once thought that merely dreaming of almonds would bring good luck. When I dream of them, it's in these delicious cookies.

Preparation time: 25 minutes

Preheat the oven to 350°F (176°C).

In the large bowl of an electric mixer or by hand, cream together the oil and sugar until well combined. Add the whole egg and the extract and beat until well blended.

In a separate bowl, stir together the ground almonds, flour, baking soda, and baking powder. Add the flour mixture to the sugar and oil mixture and blend thoroughly.

Take pinches of the dough, squeeze in your fist, and roll between your palms, making 12 2-inch (5 cm) balls. Place the balls on 2 cookie sheets about 3 inches (7.6 cm) apart. Using the bottom of a glass or pan, flatten the balls to 1/2-inch (1.2 cm) thickness. Press a whole almond gently into the center of each cookie (optional) and brush the tops of the cookies with egg yolk.

Bake in the preheated oven 10 to 12 minutes, or until the yolk wash has just begun to turn golden brown. Leave the cookies on the pan 2 to 3 minutes until they've begun to firm up, then place on a wire rack to cool completely.

Makes 12 large cookies

3/4 cup (177 ml) olive oil

1 cup (236 ml) sugar

1 large egg, plus 1 egg yolk

1 1/2 teaspoons (7.5 ml) almond extract

1/2 cup (118 ml) finely ground, blanched almonds (a blender or food processor will do this nicely)

2 cups (472 ml) unbleached, all-purpose flour

1 teaspoon (5 ml) baking soda

1 teaspoon (5 ml) baking powder

12 whole blanched almonds (optional)

Stuffed Picnic Bread with Manzanilla Olives

1 package (2 1/4 teaspoons, 11.25 ml) active dry yeast

1/2 teaspoon (2.5 ml) salt

3 to 3 1/2 cups (708 to 826 ml) unbleached bread flour or all-purpose flour

3 tablespoons (45 ml) olive oil

1/2 cup (118 ml) chopped roasted peppers (well drained and patted dry, if canned)

1/4 pound (110 g) thinly sliced Italian salami

1/4 pound (110 g) thinly sliced imported provolone

1 cup (236 ml) sliced, pitted Manzanilla olives

1 1/2 tablespoons (22.5 ml) chopped fresh oregano leaves (or 1 1/2 teaspoons, 7.5 ml, dried)

Cornmeal or additional flour

12 ice cubes

Extra virgin olive oil for drizzling (optional)

*T*his bread is an entire meal in itself. All you need is a bottle of wine and a cruet of extra virgin olive oil for drizzling, and your picnic is set—no sandwiches to make, no cold cuts to take. You can vary the fillings according to your personal taste. Any pitted olive can be substituted. You can make this bread the day before and store it wrapped in plastic. Instructions for making the dough by hand and with a bread machine are included.

Preparation time: 1 hour, plus 2-2 1/2 hours rising time

By hand: Pour 1 1/2 cups (354 ml) warm (105°-115°F, 41°-46°C) water into a large mixing bowl. Sprinkle the yeast on top, then stir to dissolve. Add the salt, 2 cups (472 ml) of the flour, 1 tablespoon (15 ml) of the olive oil, and stir to combine. Add additional flour 1/2 cup (118 ml) at a time, stirring to fully incorporate it, until a smooth soft dough is formed.

Spread some flour on a board or countertop and turn the dough out onto it. Knead the dough for about 5 minutes, adding additional flour only if needed, until the dough is smooth and elastic.

Place the dough in a large floured bowl, cover, and let rise in a warm place until it has doubled in bulk, about 55 to 75 minutes.

With a bread machine: Place 1 3/4 cups (413 ml) of water, 3 cups (708 ml) of flour, the salt, 1 tablespoon (15 ml) of the olive oil, and the yeast in the machine in the order suggested by the manufacturer. Set the machine on the dough setting. At the end of the cycle (approximately 1 hour of rising time), if the dough has not fully risen, turn the machine off and allow the dough to continue to rise until it has doubled in bulk. When you are satisfied that the dough has risen sufficiently, press start again and run the machine for about 30 seconds to punch down the dough. Proceed with the recipe.

Lightly dust a baking sheet with cornmeal or flour. Set aside.

Punch down the dough and turn it onto a floured surface. Pat or roll out the dough into a 10-inch by 15-inch (25.5 by 38 cm) rectangle. Brush the remaining olive oil evenly over the surface, leaving a 1-inch (2.5 cm) margin on each 10-inch (25.5 cm) side, and a 2-inch (5 cm) margin on the 15-inch (38 cm) side away from you.

Spread the peppers evenly over the oiled area, followed by the salami, then the provolone, then the olives, and finally the oregano, leaving the margins clear.

Starting with the long side nearest you, roll the dough up jelly-roll fashion. Pinch the long seam together, then the end seams. Fold the end seams toward the side with the long seam, and carefully roll over onto the prepared baking sheet, seam side down. Cover with a towel or plastic wrap and let it rise until it has doubled in bulk, about 45 to 50 minutes. When almost risen, preheat the oven to 425°F (218°C).

Place the bread in the preheated oven and toss 4 ice cubes onto the bottom of the oven (or in a shallow pan on the bottom of the oven), and close the door quickly.

Bake for 5 minutes, then toss in 4 more ice cubes. Bake 15 minutes longer, and toss in the last ice cubes. Bake 5 to 10 minutes longer, or until golden brown and hollow sounding when tapped. Cool completely on a wire rack. Slice and serve as is, or drizzled with extra virgin oil, if desired.

Serves 4 to 6

Nyons Olive Bread

2 1/4 cups (531 ml) water

2 tablespoons (30 ml) sugar

1 tablespoon (15 ml) grated lemon zest

1/2 teaspoon (2.5 ml) salt

1 1/2 tablespoons (7.5 ml) caraway seeds

2 teaspoons (10 ml) fennel seeds

2 packages (4 1/2 teaspoons, 22.5 ml) active dry yeast

3 1/2 to 4 1/2 cups (826 ml to 1.06 kg) bread flour or unbleached, all-purpose flour

1/4 cup plus 1 tablespoon (59 ml plus 15 ml) olive oil

2 1/2 cups (590 ml) light or medium rye flour

1 1/2 cups (354 ml) lightly packed, pitted Nyons olives halves

Corn meal

This is such a rich and flavorful bread you may want to make a meal of it. Just serve with a little butter and you've got a picnic. You may substitute oil-cured or Italian roasted olives for the Nyons.

Preparation time: 1 hour 20 minutes, plus 1 hour 45 minutes rising time

Place the water, sugar, lemon zest, salt, and seeds in a small saucepan. Bring to a boil and remove from the heat. Allow to cool to lukewarm (110° to 115°F, 43° to 46°C), then add yeast and stir to dissolve. Mix in 2 cups (472 ml) of the bread flour and the 1/4 cup (59 ml) oil. When well combined, add all the rye flour and mix well. Stir in the olives.

Add more bread flour, 1/2 cup (118 ml) at a time, until you've got a firm dough. Turn out onto a floured surface and knead for about 5 minutes, or until the dough is elastic.

Oil a large bowl with the final tablespoon (15 ml) of oil, put the dough in it, and turn to grease the top. Cover with plastic wrap and a towel and let rise in a warm place 1 hour, or until doubled in bulk. (If your kitchen isn't warm, turn on the oven at 200°F (93°C) for 1 minute, turn it off, place the bowl of dough in the oven, and close the door until risen.)

When doubled, punch dough down, knead a moment, halve, and form each half into a round loaf. Sprinkle cornmeal on 2 baking sheets, place dough on them, cover with plastic wrap and let rise until doubled, 35 to 45 minutes.

Preheat oven to 375°F (190°C).

Bake loaves in preheated oven 40 to 45 minutes, or until a knife inserted comes out clean.

Makes 2 loaves

Golden Carrot Muffins

Carrots, members of the parsley family, have been touted as health boosters for over 2,000 years. Renowned for their high vitamin A content, they're popular the world over. One of the few vegetables to have made it to the dessert course (carrot cake) and to breakfast and tea tables. The use of olive oil makes these muffins healthy, attractive, and moist.

Preparation time: 35 minutes

Preheat the oven to 400°F (204°C).

Lightly oil and flour 12 3-inch (7.5 cm) muffin cups.

In a large bowl, stir together the flour, sugar, baking powder, and salt. Add the lemon zest, raisins, and nuts, and stir well.

In a small bowl, whisk the eggs with the milk and oil until thoroughly combined. Add the wet ingredients to the dry, and stir just until no dry flour remains. Add the carrot and fold in gently until incorporated.

Spoon the batter into the prepared muffin cups, filling about 3/4 full. Bake 20 to 25 minutes, or until the muffins are lightly browned and test for doneness with a toothpick.

Makes 12 muffins

2 cups (472 ml) unbleached, all-purpose flour

1/2 cup (118 ml) sugar

1 tablespoon (15 ml) baking powder

1/2 teaspoon (2.5 ml) salt

2 teaspoons (10 ml) freshly grated lemon zest

3/4 cup (177 ml) golden raisins

3/4 cup (177 ml) walnuts or pecans

2 large eggs, or 3 large egg whites

1/2 cup (118 ml) milk

1/3 cup (79 ml) olive oil

1 1/2 cups (354 ml) gently packed, shredded carrot (about 3 medium-sized carrots)

Most Memorable Madeleines

3 egg whites

2 egg yolks

2 teaspoons (30 ml) vanilla

1 cup (236 ml) unbleached, all-purpose flour, sifted before measuring

1/2 cup (118 ml) superfine sugar

1/4 teaspoon (59 ml) salt

1/2 cup (118 ml) olive oil

A shudder ran through me and I stopped, intent upon the extra-ordinary thing that was happening to me. An exquisite pleasure had invaded my senses." So Marcel Proust describes his initial taste of a madeleine in Swann's Way, the first portion of his eight-part novel, Remembrance of Things Past. Perhaps he's a tad melodramatic, but an incredibly good madeleine can be something of an experience indeed. Light and delicate, they are perfect with a cup of tea or a dish of ice cream. Bake these in two 12-mold pans or in two shifts with one pan.

Preparation time: 25 minutes

Preheat the oven to 375°F (190°C). Oil and flour the madeleine molds.

In a small bowl, beat the egg whites until they are stiff but not dry. In a separate mixing bowl, beat together the egg yolks and vanilla. Set both bowls aside.

Sift together the sifted flour, sugar, and salt. Beat 1/3 of the flour mixture into the egg yolks. Mix thoroughly. Add 1/4 cup (118 ml) of the oil and beat to mix well. Add another 1/3 of the flour, the rest of the oil, then the last of the flour, beating well after each addition.

Fold 1/3 of the egg whites into the batter to loosen and thin it. Gently fold in the remaining whites until well combined. Spoon the batter into the prepared molds, filling about 2/3 full.

Bake for 10 minutes, or until firm when lightly pressed and the edges are just turning golden brown. Turn out onto a wire rack to cool completely. Store in an airtight container.

Makes 24 madeleines

Olive Identifier

Olive flavors are affected by lots of factors, even within the same variety—the climate where they're grown; when they're picked and how; when they're brined and for how long; whether they're packed in herbs, oils, or other flavorings; how long they've been on the shelf or in the merchant's crock; and the temperature at which they've been stored, to name a few. Nevertheless, here is a list of the variety of olives that are readily available at local supermarkets, gourmet shops, and by mail order:

AGRINION
Huge, Greek, dull green, slit, and brine cured, with sour taste and very soft flesh. Flesh easily torn from the pit.

ALPHONSO
Huge Chilean variety, pale brown to bright purple, brine-cured, then wine- or wine vinegar-cured, with soft, somewhat bitter flesh. Easy to pit.

ARBEQUINA
Quite small, reddish-green, brine-cured Spanish variety with somewhat tough skin, little flesh, crunchy bite, and sharp, bitter, faintly smoky taste. Hard to pit. Primarily used for oil, but sometimes sold cured with stems and even leaves attached.

ATALANTA
Medium-sized, greenish-brown, Greek-type, with soft, meaty flesh, and full, earthy flavor. One of few European olives sold already pitted.

BARESI DOLCI
Medium-sized, elongated, dull green, ash-cured variety from Apulian area of Italy, with a crisp texture and a delicate, surprisingly sweet taste. Hard to pit.

BELLA DI CERIGNOLA BLACK
Huge jet black southern Italian variety, ash-cured, with soft flesh and delicately sweet taste. More flavorful and easier to pit than the green version.

BELLA DI CERIGNOLA GREEN
Enormous blue-green, southern Italian variety, ash-cured to produce sweet, dense, vegetablelike flesh. Hard to pit.

CALIFORNIAN SICILIAN-STYLE
Very large, dull green, brine-cured, similar to Sevillano, with crisp bite. Sometimes cracked. Hard to pit.

CHINESE PRESERVED
Eaten like candy in China. Medium to large, shriveled, elongated, with pointed ends, brown to golden color, cured with salt, sugar, honey, or licorice root. Sweet and salty with a licorice taste. "Less candied" varieties easy to pit is steamed or boiled to soften flesh.

CHINESE SALTED
Pale green, cracked, brine-cured variety from Provence, with firm flesh. Usually marinated with herbs. Easy to pit.

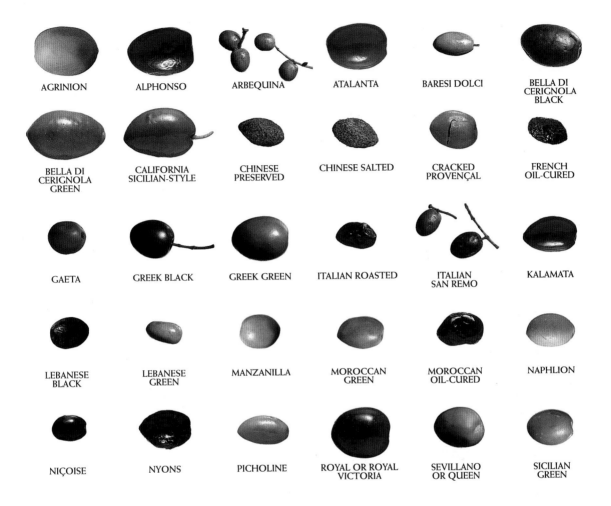

AGRINION ALPHONSO ARBEQUINA ATALANTA BARESI DOLCI BELLA DI CERIGNOLA BLACK

BELLA DI CERIGNOLA GREEN CALIFORNIA SICILIAN-STYLE CHINESE PRESERVED CHINESE SALTED CRACKED PROVENÇAL FRENCH OIL-CURED

GAETA GREEK BLACK GREEK GREEN ITALIAN ROASTED ITALIAN SAN REMO KALAMATA

LEBANESE BLACK LEBANESE GREEN MANZANILLA MOROCCAN GREEN MOROCCAN OIL-CURED NAPHLION

NIÇOISE NYONS PICHOLINE ROYAL OR ROYAL VICTORIA SEVILLANO OR QUEEN SICILIAN GREEN

FRENCH OIL-CURED

Sleek, black, wrinkled. Similar in appearance to Nyons, with intense taste reminiscent of whiskey. Easy to pull apart and remove pit.

GAETA

Small Italian variety, sometimes black, wrinkled and salt-cured, sometimes smooth purple and brine-cured. Flavorful, sour, salty, and sometimes hard to pit.

GREEK BLACK

Large, dark brown to purple type, with soft pulp and a flavor reminiscent of red wine. Easy to pit.

GREEK GREEN

Fat, juicy, pale green variety. Somewhat acrid and easy to pit.

ITALIAN ROASTED

Oven-dried Southern Italian variety, sometimes with smoky flavor, salty, moist, glossy black, intense, with a hint of cinnamon in the taste. Easy to pull apart.

ITALIAN SAN REMO

Small variety, ranging in color from greenish-brown to purplish-black, relatively low in sodium, with delicate artichokelike flavor, and lingering vegetable aftertaste. Often sold in herb infused oil. Hard to pit.

KALAMATA

Also spelled Calamata. Smooth, medium-sized, bullet-shaped Greek variety, with intense after-taste. Slit, brine-cured, and usually packed in vinegar. Easy to pit.

LEBANESE BLACK

Smooth, medium-sized, glossy brown to black, with a pleasant, though intense, earthy taste, but slightly meaty flesh. Squeeze to open and pit pops out.

MANZANILLA

Small to medium-sized green variety with crisp flesh and slightly smoky flavor—a mainstay of both the Spanish and California industries. Easy to pit but frequently sold pitted and often stuffed with reconstituted pimento.

MOROCCAN GREEN

Salty, cracked variety with softer flesh than most green olives and full tart taste. Easy to pit, delightful.

MOROCCAN OIL-CURED

Probably the best of the type, which is also called dry-cured and salt-cured. Glistening, jet black, medium-sized, meaty, and slightly bitter, with a smoky taste that lingers. Moister ones are easy to pit by pulling apart.

NAPHLION

Also spelled several other ways. Medium-sized, glossy, dark green to brown variety, that's cracked, brine-cured, and usually packed in oil. Has an intense, salty-sour flavor. A crisp snap and can be pulled from the pit.

NIÇOISE

Small, dark brownish-purple French variety, with sharp, somewhat sour taste and a large pit. Often packed with herbs. Hard to pit.

NYONS

Small, greenish-black to jet black variety from southern France, with a pleasantly bitter taste, usually dry-cured and dressed, but a few are brine-cured. Easy to pull apart and pit.

PICHOLINE

Long, pointy, pale green, brine-cured French variety, usually packed in citric acid in the U.S. Sweet, crunchy texture, and slight saltiness. A cocktail favorite, but its pit is hard to remove.

ROYAL OR ROYAL VICTORIA

Enormous, varying from dark red to light brown, this Greek variety is slit, brine-cured, and often packed in oil and vinegar, with soft flesh and pungent aftertaste. Easy to pit.

SEVILLANO OR QUEEN

Huge, bland, brine-cures, medium-green variety, grown in California and Spain. Usually marketed in U.S. as "Super-Colossal." Hard to pit.

SICILIAN GREEN

Large, pale, brownish-green, with assertive sour taste and dense flesh. Easy to pit if brined for a while.

Index